# TEACHING
# ARCHERY

## Steps to Success

**Kathleen M. Haywood, PhD**
University of Missouri—St. Louis

**Catherine F. Lewis, MEd**
Andrews Academy
Creve Coeur, Missouri

**Leisure Press**
Champaign, Illinois

**Library of Congress Cataloging-in-Publication Data**

Haywood, Kathleen.
    Teaching archery: steps to success / Kathleen M. Haywood,
Catherine F. Lewis.
        p. cm.—(Steps to success activity series)
    Bibliography: p.
    ISBN 0-88011-334-0
    1. Archery—Study and teaching. I. Lewis, Catherine, 1957-
II. Title. III. Series.
GV1184.54H39  1989
799.3'2'07—dc19                                                                    88-9429
                                                                                   CIP


Developmental Editor: Judy Patterson Wright, PhD
Production Director: Ernie Noa
Copy Editor: Peter Nelson
Assistant Editor: Kathy Kane
Proofreader: Laurie McGee
Typesetter: Yvonne Winsor
Text Design: Keith Blomberg
Text Layout: Tara Welsch
Cover Design: Jack Davis
Cover Photo: Bill Morrow
Illustrations By: Pam Shaver and Gretchen Walters
Printed By: Phillips Brothers Printers

ISBN: 0-88011-334-0

Printed in the United States of America

10  9  8  7  6  5  4  3  2  1

**Leisure Press**
A Division of Human Kinetics Publishers, Inc.
Box 5076, Champaign, IL 61820
1-800-342-5457
1-800-334-3665 (in Illinois)

# Contents

# Series Preface

The Steps to Success Activity Series is a breakthrough in skill instruction through the development of complete learning progressions—the *steps to success*. These *steps* help students quickly perform basic skills successfully and prepare them to acquire advanced skills readily. At each step, students are encouraged to learn at their own pace and to integrate their new skills into the total action of the activity, which motivates them to achieve.

The unique features of the Steps to Success Activity Series are the result of comprehensive development—through analyzing existing activity books, incorporating the latest research from the sport sciences and consulting with students, instructors, teacher educators, and administrators. This groundwork pointed up the need for three different types of books—for participants, instructors, and teacher educators—which we have created and together comprise the Steps to Success Activity Series.

The *participant book* for each activity is a self-paced, step-by-step guide; learners can use it as a primary resource for a beginning activity class or as a self-instructional guide. The unique features of each *step* in the participant book include

- sequential illustrations that clearly show proper technique for all basic skills,
- helpful suggestions for detecting and correcting errors,
- excellent drill progressions with accompanying *Success Goals* for measuring performance, and
- a complete checklist for each basic skill for a trained observer to rate the learner's technique.

A comprehensive *instructor guide* accompanies the participant's book for each activity, emphasizing how to individualize instruction. Each *step* of the instructor's guide promotes successful teaching and learning with

- teaching cues (*Keys to Success*) that emphasize fluidity, rhythm, and wholeness,

- criterion-referenced rating charts for evaluating a participant's initial skill level,
- suggestions for observing and correcting typical errors,
- tips for group management and safety,
- ideas for adapting every drill to increase or decrease the difficulty level,
- quantitative evaluations for all drills (*Success Goals*), and
- a complete test bank of written questions.

The series textbook, *Instructional Design for Teaching Physical Activities*, explains the *steps to success* model, which is the basis for the Steps to Success Activity Series. Teacher educators can use this text in their professional preparation classes to help future teachers and coaches learn how to design effective physical activity programs in school, recreation, or community teaching and coaching settings.

After identifying the need for participant, instructor, and teacher educator texts, we refined the *steps to success* instructional design model and developed prototypes for the participant and the instructor books. Once these prototypes were fine-tuned, we carefully selected authors for the activities who were not only thoroughly familiar with their sports but had years of experience in teaching them. Each author had to be known as a gifted instructor who understands the teaching of sport so thoroughly that he or she could readily apply the *steps to success* model.

Next, all of the participant and instructor manuscripts were carefully developed to meet the guidelines of the *steps to success* model. Then our production team, along with outstanding artists, created a highly visual, user-friendly series of books.

*The result*: The Steps to Success Activity Series is the premier sports instructional series available today. The participant books are the best available for helping you to become a master player, the instructor guides will help you to become a master teacher, and the teacher educator's text prepares you to design your own programs.

This series would not have been possible without the contributions of the following:

- Dr. Joan Vickers, instructional design expert,
- Dr. Rainer Martens, Publisher,
- the staff of Human Kinetics Publishers, and

- the *many* students, teachers, coaches, consultants, teacher educators, specialists, and administrators who shared their ideas—and dreams.

Judy Patterson Wright
Series Editor

We have each occasionally had the experience of observing someone else teaching archery, either formally or informally, only to cause us to turn away and say, "I wish I had those students for just an hour; I'd have them. . . ." Perhaps you have found yourself saying this, even in regard to another sport.

We spend a good deal of time shooting archery and enjoy the challenge of shooting. Naturally, we are anxious for beginning archers to have successful experiences so that they can enjoy the sport as much as we do. For these initial experiences to be positive ones, beginners must feel they are making progress.

We meet many people whose first experiences with archery were in school or camp programs. They often recount to us that the one thing they remember was hitting their forearm with the bowstring and how much it hurt, or missing the whole target when they shot. Our goal in writing this book has been to help teachers provide archery students with positive experiences during which they could see progress and come to feel they were mastering the sport. We joined the *Steps to Success* writing team because we believed using the model for the *Steps to Success* series would provide the best archery instruction resource available.

What is unique to this book compared to the archery resources available before is the progression of lessons beyond the first few days of class and through an entire course. The archery equivalents of skill drills are provided to give students practice, but also to prepare them to move on to further aspects of archery. The approach here is distinctly different from teaching students the basic shot in the first few days of classes, then simply letting them shoot for the remainder of the course.

In brief, we have stressed the use of mimicking at the outset; minimizing accessories, particularly the bowsight, in early lessons; short distances and large targets at the start; and de-emphasizing scoring until good form develops. Early practices include partner activities, recognizing that students may tire if they shoot continuously in early lessons. Once sound basic form is attained, accessories are introduced, the students are moved farther from the target, the targets used are smaller, and more emphasis is placed on scoring. The students are given an opportunity to experiment with varying several components of the archery shot to develop their best personal styles; and the mental approach to performance, such a pivotal aspect of this sport, is introduced.

We have also emphasized the fitting of equipment and steps instructors can take to provide the necessary accessories at little cost. There is probably no other sport that surpasses archery in the strong tie between the equipment provided students and their potential for attaining high absolute levels of scoring performance. In this text we have allowed for instructors who are fortunate enough to have nearly ideal equipment and facility resources. However, we have tried to keep in mind that the majority have less than this ideal, and to show how equipment limitations need not stop the instructional process.

We would like to thank our archery friends who were happy to "talk archery" and help us learn more and more about the sport and about teaching it. There is always something new to learn, particularly in regard to equipment as new materials become available to archery manufacturers. We would also like to thank the Arrow Point Archery staff and Melinda Kerr with her class of physical education majors at the University of Missouri-St. Louis, who let us take photographs that were then provided to our artist to best illustrate this text.

Kathleen M. Haywood

Catherine F. Lewis

# Implementing the Steps to Success Staircase

This book is meant to be flexible not only to your students' needs but to your needs as well. It is common to hear that students' perceptions of a task change as the task is learned. However, we often forget that teachers' perceptions and actions also change (Goc-Karp & Zakrajsek, 1987; Housner & Griffey, 1985; Imwold & Hoffman, 1983).

More experienced or master teachers tend to approach the teaching of activities in a similar manner. They are highly organized (e.g., they do not waste time getting groups together or use long explanations); they integrate information (e.g., from biomechanics, kinesiology, exercise physiology, motor learning, sport psychology, cognitive psychology, instructional design, and etc.); and they relate basic skills into the larger game or performance context. This includes succinctly explaining why the basic skills, concepts, or tactics are important within the game or performance setting (e.g., tournaments). Then, usually within a few minutes, their students are placed into practice situations that progress in steps that follow logical manipulations of factors such as

- the addition or removal of equipment,
- spacial restriction or availability, and
- the size and distance of targets.

This book will show you how the basic archery skills, equipment, and selected physiological, psychological, and other pertinent knowledge are interrelated (see Appendix A for an overview). You can use this information not only to gain insights into the various interrelationships but also to define the subject matter for archery. The following questions offer specific suggestions for implementing this knowledge base and help you to evaluate and improve your teaching methods, which include class organization, drills, objectives, progressions, and evaluations.

1. Under what conditions do you teach?
   - How much space is available?
   - What type of equipment is available? It may be necessary to construct some of your own equipment. See the guidelines on how to construct your own target stands and arrow cart in Appendix B and how to construct a box bow stringer in Appendix C.
   - What is the average class size?
   - How much time is allotted per class session?
   - How many class sessions do you teach?
   - Do you have any teaching assistants?

2. What are your students' initial skill levels?
   - Look for the rating charts located in the beginning of most steps, or chapters, to identify the criteria that discriminate between beginning, intermediate, and advanced skill levels.

3. What is the best order to teach archery skills?
   - Follow the sequence of steps (chapters) used in this book.
   - See Appendix D.1 for suggestions on when to introduce, review, or continue practicing each step.
   - Based on your answers to the previous questions, use the form in Appendix D.2 to order the steps that you will be able to cover in the time available.

4. What objectives do you want your students to accomplish by the end of a lesson, unit, or course?
   - For your technique or qualitative objectives, select from the Student Keys to Success (or the Keys to Success Checklists in *Archery: Steps to Success*) that are provided for all basic skills.

- For your performance or quantitative objectives, select from the Success Goals provided for each drill.
- For written questions on safety, rules, technique, equipment, history, and psychological aspects of archery, select from the Test Bank of written questions.
- See the Sample Individual Program (Appendix E.1) for selected technique and performance objectives for a 16-week unit.
- For unit objectives, adjust your total number of selected objectives to fit your unit length (use the form in Appendix E.2).
- For organizing daily objectives, see the Sample Lesson Plan in Appendix F.1, and modify the basic lesson plan form in Appendix F.2 to best fit your needs.

5. How will you evaluate your students?

- Read the section on Evaluation Ideas.
- Decide on your type of grading system, for example, letter grades, pass-fail, total points, percentages, skill levels (bronze, silver, gold), and so forth.

6. Which activities should be selected to achieve student objectives?

- Follow the drills and/or exercises for each step because they are specifically designed for large groups of students and are presented in a planned, easy-to-difficult order. Avoid a random approach to selecting drills and exercises.
- Modify drills as necessary to best fit your students' skill levels by following the suggestions for decreasing and increasing the difficulty level of each drill.
- Ask students to meet the Success Goal listed for each drill.
- Use the cross-reference to the corresponding step and drill number within the participants' book, *Archery: Steps to Success*, for class assignments or makeups.

7. What rules and expectations do you have for your class?

- For general management and safety guidelines, read the section "Preparing Your Class for Success."
- For specific guidelines, read the section "Group Management and Safety Tips" included with each drill.
- Let your students know what your rules are during your class orientation and/or first day of class. Then post them and repeat them often.

Teaching is a complex task, requiring you to make many decisions that will affect both you and your students (see Figure 1). Use this book to create an effective and successful learning experience for you and everyone you teach. And remember, have fun too!

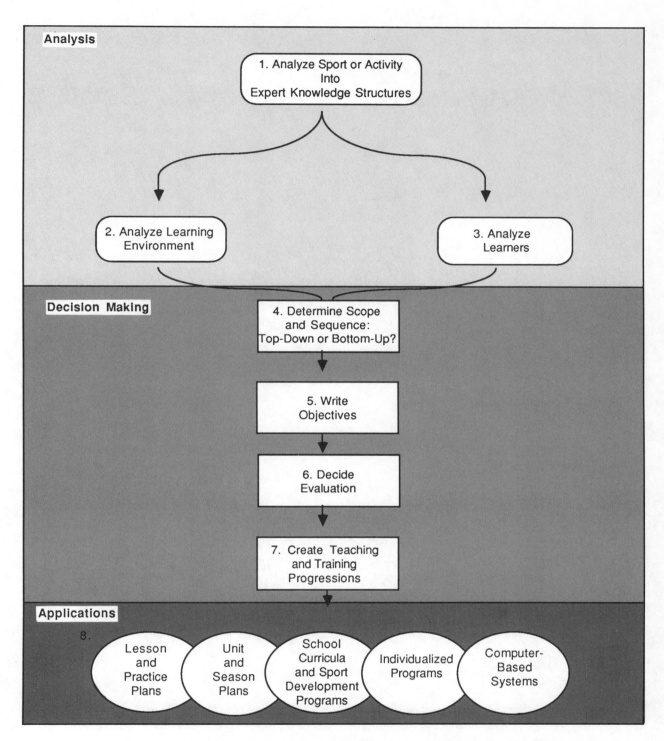

**Figure 1: Instructional design model utilizing expert knowledge structures.**

**Figure 1** Instructional design model utilizing expert knowledge structures. *Note.* From *Instructional Design for Teaching Physical Activities* by J.N. Vickers, in press, Champaign, IL: Human Kinetics. Copyright by Joan N. Vickers. Reprinted by permission. This instructional design model has appeared in earlier forms in *Badminton: A Structures of Knowledge Approach* (p. 1) by J.N. Vickers and D. Brecht, 1987, Calgary, AB: University Printing Services. Copyright 1987 by Joan N. Vickers; and "The Role of Expert Knowledge Structures in an Instructional Design Model for Physical Education" by J.N. Vickers, 1983, *Journal of Teaching in Physical Education*, **2**(3), p. 20. Copyright 1983 by Joan N. Vickers.

# Preparing Your Class for Success

Before you begin teaching your archery classes, you need to make many procedural decisions. These hinge on whether you will teach indoors, outdoors, or both, depending upon the weather. You will need to organize your range and decide what preparations of your range are necessary on a daily basis. You must then decide what general patterns will be followed every day the class is held, and then how to organize individual classes to make them run efficiently. The following items give you guidance in creating an effective learning environment.

## GENERAL CLASS MANAGEMENT

The first decision you will make pertains to the operation of your classes on a day-in, day-out basis. Establish the general pattern to follow every day. You may wish to consider the following points:

- Decide how students will pick up their equipment on a daily basis. You may have them report to the storage area to pick up their equipment and carry it to the shooting range, or you may transport it to the shooting range yourself. If you decide upon the latter, you will probably need to have an equipment cart made. A suggestion for one is included in Appendix B.
- Make arrangements for inclement weather days if you plan to shoot outdoors. Be sure your students know that an indoor range is available if it is, or that you have classes planned for indoors. As an example of the latter, you could teach equipment maintenance during inclement weather; students need to know where to report on such days.
- Decide whether or not your students will be responsible for some aspects of equipment storage at the end of class. Estimate how much time must be allotted for this, so students will not be late for their next appointments.

- If you plan to use any audiovisual or video equipment in your archery course, reserve it well in advance so that you will be sure to have it for the appropriate lesson.
- When successive archery classes are taught, remember not to leave shooting equipment on the range unattended between classes.
- Make arrangements to transport target butts to the range if necessary. If maintenance personnel will take care of this, provide a schedule of days and times that targets are needed. If students will help, plan how to move the equipment, such as on a hand truck, using tripod stands as "stretchers," and so on.

## CLASS ORGANIZATION TECHNIQUES

In conducting daily classes you should establish practices that minimize your organization time and maximize your instruction time. Here are some suggestions:

- Number or code all of the archery equipment so that your students can find their equipment with a minimum of confusion. Record equipment assignments. You may even want to post these assignments at the equipment storage cabinet or on your equipment cart in case students forget their assignments.
- Use a signal, such as a whistle, to begin and end shooting and to have students retrieve their arrows. Be sure your students know the emergency stop signal and practice use of it in nonemergency situations. You may also want to teach your students to ease their shots down at your verbal command, "let down." This command can be used with an individual student if you detect that something is wrong, such as an arrow having slipped off the string, while coaching the student.

1

- Have students mimic aspects of technique without equipment or with fewer pieces of equipment. Take this opportunity to correct aspects of form before their attention is shifted to manipulating their equipment.
- Hold to a minimum the number of teaching points presented to a class at one time. Allow your students to implement these points before you add more.
- Let your students practice a new technique or reminder as soon as practical after your explanation or demonstration.
- Use partner monitoring early in the course. Extra eyes can be beneficial to the instructional process, and students may tire quickly if they shoot continuously, anyway. Students become involved in technique at another level when they are challenged to observe their partners, and this makes them more knowledgeable. If students must share equipment, monitoring keeps them on task between shooting periods.

**CLASS WARM-UPS FOR ARCHERY**

Stretching the arm, neck, and upper trunk muscles prepares students for shooting. Regular strengthening exercises also help to improve students' strength for shooting with bows of sufficient poundage to facilitate scoring success. Have your students take a position along the shooting line. If the number of students is large, two or more lines can be formed. Position yourself in front of the students, downrange.

One or two minutes of vigorous activity warms the muscles and reduces the likelihood of injury during stretching. Assuming that space is limited, begin your exercise warm-up with jumping jacks, rope jumping, or jogging in place. You can alternate among these from session to session.

Lead the following exercises next. A description of how they are performed can be found in *Archery: Steps to Success*. Remind students to stretch slowly into position until they feel the pull, to hold the position, then ease back slowly.

1. Hugs
2. Arm circles
3. Arm stretches
4. Hand clasps
5. Up-and-down hand clasps
6. Trunk twists
7. Neck stretches

The following strength exercises are designed to be used on the shooting range without extensive weight-training equipment. Descriptions of each strength exercise can be found in *Archery: Steps to Success*. Resistance can be provided in two ways. You can have students pair up with someone approximately equal in strength, alternately resisting the partner's movement. Otherwise, you can use Spri Xercise Tubing® if you have enough for each student in class; it comes in three strengths (levels of resistance) to accommodate students' initial strength levels. Look for students to have weaker back muscles than shoulder and chest muscles.

1. Back pulls
2. Chest pulls
3. Frontal plane pulls
4. Archery draw pulls

**EQUIPMENT FOR SHOOTING**

Equipment needs are more extensive for archery than many other sports. However, wise purchasing provides you with equipment that will last for years. Some equipment can be made very inexpensively, and taking the time to make it allows your students to shoot using accessories from which they otherwise would not benefit. Table F.1 lists the equipment needed for a class of 24 students. In some cases more than 24 of an item should be purchased so that you can accommodate a range of student sizes and strengths, that is, so that you can fit your students properly. You can narrow the range of your purchases if you teach in a setting that has a minimum of these variations; for instance, for classes of women only, you can order less heavy or long equipment. Settings with a larger proportion of taller and stronger individuals calls for less light or short equipment. If your setting has a maximum of these variations, it is wise to purchase even more equipment than usual. You should also purchase extras of some items that are subject to breakage.

Here are some special considerations to keep in mind when selecting types or styles of equipment.

**1. *Bows:*** It is best to purchase recurve bows if at all possible. The working limbs of a recurve bow provide more thrust and allow the student to shoot in a flatter arc and from longer distances. The cutout sight window, making the bow closer to center shot, permits the student to shoot without having to compensate for the arrow sitting at an angle. Both of these factors promote more accurate shooting.

Most one-piece recurve bows on the market are laminated wood and fiberglass. A bow of this type is your most likely purchase because take-down bows with metal handle risers are typically beyond the price range of most educational programs. Buy the best quality you can afford. Purchase a variety of lengths from 62–66 inches if possible, generally combining shorter lengths with lighter poundage and longer lengths with heavier poundage.

**2. *Bow Tip Protectors:*** A bow tip protector is not a necessity, but it helps protect the tip of the lower limb, over which it is placed (see Figure F.1). Moreover, it keeps the bowstring attached to the bow when it is not strung, minimizing the chance of losing the bowstring or having bowstrings interchanged on various bows.

**Table F.1 Recommended Equipment Inventory for Classes of 24 Students**

| Item | Quantity | Size or description |
|------|----------|---------------------|
| Right-handed bows | 3 | 15-pound |
| | 8 | 20-pound |
| | 8 | 25-pound |
| | 3 | 30-pound |
| | 2 | 35-pound |
| Left-handed bows | 1 | 15-pound |
| | 2 | 20-pound |
| | 2 | 25-pound |
| | 1 | 30-pound |
| Bow tip protectors | 1 per bow | |
| Arm guards | 24 | Regular length |
| | 6 | Long length |
| Finger tabs | 10 | Right-hand, small |
| | 10 | Right-hand, medium |
| | 8 | Right-hand, large |
| | 3 | Left-hand, small |
| | 3 | Left-hand, medium |
| | 2 | Left-hand, large |
| Quivers | 28 | |

| Item | Quantity | Size or description |
|------|----------|---------------------|
| Bow slings | 10 | Small |
| | 10 | Medium |
| | 8 | Large |
| Bowsights | 28 | |
| Arrow rests | 32 | Right-hand |
| | 8 | Left-hand |
| Nock locators | 36 | 8- and 10-strand |
| Clothing shields | 6 | Right-hand, small |
| | 7 | Right-hand, medium |
| | 7 | Right-hand, large |
| | 2 | Left-hand, small |
| | 3 | Left-hand, medium |
| | 3 | Left-hand, large |
| Stabilizers* | 26 | 30 inches |

*Needed only if bows are tapped to accept a stabilizer

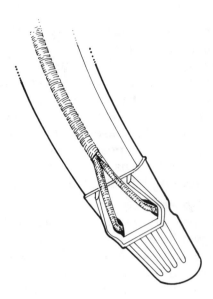

**Figure F.1**  Bow tip protectors not only protect the limb tip but keep bowstrings with bows when they are unstrung between classes.

**3. Arrow Rests:** If you are able to furnish recurve bows to your students, you should purchase arrow rests if they are not included with the bows. Better styles have a contact point that gives when the arrow pushes against it at release, that is, the contact point is cushioned. Most arrow rests are delicate, and beginners can be hard on them. For example, if a beginner pinches the arrow nock between the fingers and pushes down on the arrow, the arrow in turn pushes down on the arrow rest. If maintaining arrow rests is problematic with your students, you might consider purchasing arrow rests made for hunting conditions, because they are more durable.

**4. Bowsights:** A bowsight that mounts onto the back of the bow is sufficient for the beginning archery student. Several inexpensive styles are available. Purchasing a style with a durable aiming aperture is cost effective because a delicate aperture model, especially those mounted by a relatively thin wire, is likely to be easily damaged with class use.

**5. Bow Slings:** The type of bow sling you purchase is largely a matter of preference. Finger slings are particularly inexpensive, but styles that attach to the bow are not easily lost, and they adjust in size.

**6. Arm Guards:** Arm guards come in a variety of styles. All serve their purpose well, but those that have slits or openings are much cooler in hot weather. In class settings, plastic styles and those that slip over the arm are more durable than leather styles and those that have Velcro closures.

**7. Finger Tabs:** Finger tabs are the protection of choice in most educational programs. Shooting gloves are available, but they are not often used because of the excess leather placed in contact with the string. For educational programs, expense is a major factor in selecting tabs over gloves. Plastic tabs with a special lubricated surface are available. They are more costly, but they are more durable for class settings than leather tabs.

**8. Quivers:** If your class is to be held outdoors, ground quivers should be your first choice. In addition to holding arrows, a quiver usually has a bracket that holds a bow not in use. This keeps the bow off the ground, where it is likely to be stepped on or where moisture can affect it. If you are shooting indoors, you can choose between belt or floor quivers. Inexpensive belt quivers are available, or you can make them from golf club divider tubes. You can make a floor quiver from PVC pipe, a simple wooden base, and two or three L-brackets (see Figure F.2).

**Figure F.2**  Indoor ground quivers can be made from PVC pipe, a wood base, and 3 L-brackets.

**9. Arrows:** Table F.2 gives a recommendation for an ideal arrow inventory. As you will see in Step 1, beginners are best initially fitted with slightly longer arrows. As they solidify their form, they should be refitted with slightly shorter arrows to obtain better arrow flight.

**Table F.2  Recommended Arrow Inventory**

| Type | No. of dozens | Shaft size | Length (inches) |
|------|---------------|------------|-----------------|
| Aluminum | 1 | 1416 | 24 |
| | 2 | 1516 | 25 |
| | 2 | 1516 | 26 |
| | 1 | 1616 | 26 |
| | 3 | 1616 | 27 |
| | 1 | 1616 | 28 |
| | 2 | 1716 | 27 |
| | 3 | 1716 | 28 |
| | 3 | 1716 | 29 |
| | 1 | 1816 | 28 |
| | 2 | 1816 | 29 |
| | 3 | 1816 | 30 |
| | 1 | 1916 | 29 |
| | 1 | 1916 | 30 |
| | 2 | 1916 | 31 |
| | 1 | 2018 | 32 |
| Fiberglass | 1 | 0 | 24 |
| | 1 | 0 | 25 |
| | 1 | 1 | 25 |
| | 1 | 1 | 26 |
| | 2 | 2 | 26 |
| | 1 | 2 | 27 |
| | 2 | 3 | 27 |
| | 1 | 3 | 28 |
| | 2 | 4 | 27 |
| | 2 | 4 | 28 |
| | 1 | 4 | 29 |
| | 2 | 5 | 28 |
| | 3 | 5 | 29 |
| | 2 | 6 | 29 |
| | 2 | 6 | 30 |
| | 2 | 7 | 30 |
| | 1 | 7 | 31 |
| | 2 | 8 | 31 |
| Wood | 1 | < 35 lb | 24 |
| | 5 | < 35 lb | 26 |
| | 10 | < 35 lb | 28 |
| | 11 | < 35 lb | 30 |
| | 3 | 30–40 lb | 31 1/2 |

The table takes this refitting into account. Obviously, you can adapt the recommendation to fit your budget and other needs. The following points should be kept in mind when obtaining arrows for your program:

- Although a wooden arrow is by far the least expensive type of arrow, a crack in a wooden shaft necessitates that it be taken out of use. An aluminum arrow, on the other hand, can be straightened if bent. As you can see from Table F.2, aluminum and fiberglass arrows can be purchased in a wider variety of sizes to match individual archers better.
- Arrows should be purchased with target points and should be 3-fletched. A wide variety of color schemes (of fletching, nocks, and/or cresting) should be purchased so that having as many as four students shooting at the same target face at one time will still not result in arrows being mixed up. Feathers are less expensive than vanes and are considered to be more forgiving of release errors, but are not as durable or consistent as vanes.
- Shorter arrows of approximately 28 inches or less perform well with shorter fletching of 2 1/2–3 inches. Longer arrows usually necessitate slightly longer fletching, with 4 inches generally being sufficient for class use.
- Damaged arrows can be saved so that students can practice maintenance with these arrows rather than new ones.
- Purchase extra target tips and nocks in the appropriate sizes for your arrows. You will probably want a variety of nock colors to keep the arrows assigned to an individual archer alike. If you have your own fletching jig, you need fletching in various colors and sizes to match those already on the arrows.

Accessories that you need for your program follow, with the recommended multiple quantities in parentheses. The most important items are marked with asterisks.

- Bow square* (3)
- Nocking pliers*

- Pocket knife with dull blade*
- Fletching jig
- Serving jig and serving thread
- Waxed dental floss*
- Bowstring wax* (2 pieces)
- Fletching cement* (3 tubes)
- Ferrule cement
- Bow stringers (1 permanent and/or at least 3 cord stringers)
- Clipboards (6)

Later steps in this text—especially Step 6, "Adding Basic Accessories"—list additional items necessary for you to install or make other equipment.

## EQUIPMENT FOR THE SHOOTING RANGE

The size and arrangement of the shooting range often determines how many students can be accommodated in an archery class. Here we assume that six target butts are available in a size that allows four archers to shoot at each target.

Perhaps the ideal shooting range is a permanent one that remains set up. However, this is the exception rather than the rule, and some consideration must thus be given to the ease of transporting target butts.

If your class will be held outdoors on a temporary range for the majority of class sessions, the ideal target butts are circular ones constructed of Indian cord grass fibers. The best style is self-healing and is chemically treated to resist fungus and dry rot. The center is reinforced. Such target butts can last 10 or more years if properly maintained.

The 50-inch size is ideal for beginning classes and is also suitable for tournaments. You may elect to purchase 36- or 40-inch targets if they must be carried to the range daily. This may necessitate keeping students at shorter shooting distances.

A large target butt can be placed on a tripod stand or a portable, metal support with wheels (see Figure F.3). A wooden tripod is very sturdy and holds the target several feet above the ground. A portable stand holds the target very near the ground. Arrows striking the metal will probably suffer more damage

than those hitting a wooden stand. However, a metal stand can be easily wheeled from storage to shooting range, and the target butt does not have to be lifted into place. Any stand should be anchored to the ground, and targets anchored to the stand, particularly in windy conditions, to prevent a target from tipping and damaging all the arrows in it.

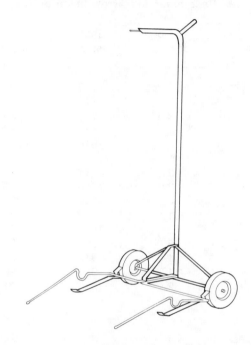

**Figure F.3** Target butt stands with wheels make transportation of target butts easy.

If your outdoor shooting range is a permanent facility, excelsior (not straw) bales are likely to be the target butt of choice. About three large bales, one on top of the other and tightly banded, make a sufficiently large target butt. Permanent stands can be made of wood or metal with a wooden backing. It is best to place a layer of thick rubber between the excelsior and the backing, and to cover exposed metal with rubber. Arrows hitting a hard surface can bounce off and reverse their direction because of the heavy tip, particularly when shot from light-poundage bows.

If your class is held indoors or if you have an inclement-weather teaching station, grass target butts can be used on the same types of stands discussed above. You can also make target butts from cardboard that is cut, stacked with the cut edges facing the shooting line, and banded. Pieces of 3/4-inch plywood at the top and bottom add strength. Sections of the target butt that become worn can be cut out and plugged with new cardboard. A wooden tripod can be used to support these cardboard targets.

Nylon backstop nets may be needed for indoor shooting ranges. These nets stop arrows that miss the targets, protecting both the surroundings and the arrows. A variety of sizes are available, and the netting will last for many years. Any hard surface, particularly of metal, should be padded or behind netting. Be prepared for novice archers to shoot arrows along the floor. If the flooring must be protected, place a tarp down for indoor shooting.

The size of your target butts may dictate the size of the target faces you need for your class. For beginners, usually the larger the target face, the better, because your students will more often feel success from hitting the target. In fact, the early shooting activities in this text often make use of handmade targets on large paper. Official target faces should be ordered for eventual use, including for a class tournament. Ideally, target butts should be large enough for 122-cm target faces to be used early in the course and for shooting from longer distances. When students are more skilled and shooting with bowsights, 80-cm target faces are challenging.

The number of target faces needed for a class depends on the quality ordered. Target faces can be ordered with crisscrossed reinforcing fibers, on heavy paper, or on lighter paper. Some are "skirted," that is, they are sewn to a gauze material that wraps around a grass fiber butt and is pulled tight with a string. Obviously, these can be used only in the size matching that of the target butt.

To some extent, the choice of target faces is a trade-off. The reinforced or heavier faces last longer, but they cost more. Instructors often experiment to find the combination most practical for them. It is best to initially err in getting more target faces than necessary, because extras can be kept for subsequent courses. At minimum, two reinforced faces should be on hand for each target butt.

Bale pins are needed to anchor target faces to the target butt, except in the case of skirted target faces. Several types of plastic bale pins can be purchased, including some that lock into place with a quarter turn. Purchase eight bale pins for each target butt available to you, plus a few extra.

You can also make bale pins from coat hangers. Begin with a straight 8-inch piece of metal cut from the hanger. Bend it approximately 2 inches from the end at a right angle and bend it around. This forms a handle (see Figure F.4). It is good to dip the handle in plastic coating liquid to prevent scratches from the end of the metal when the pin is pushed into the target. You can sharpen the other end on a bench grinder.

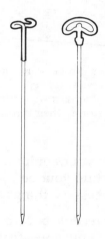

**Figure F.4** Bale pins anchor target faces to the target butt.

## EQUIPMENT PREPARATION

Before your archery course begins, you should inspect all your equipment to make sure it is in safe working order. Replacements should be purchased for damaged equipment that you cannot repair.

You should also number the equipment. You can use a permanent felt marker on many items, such as arm guards. You may prefer to place tape on some equipment, such as bows, and write on the tape. Arrows should be grouped by shaft size and length and then by color scheme. Each arrow set should then be given a number. Place this number on the storage container. For example, if arrows are stored in a wooden box (see Figure F.5), place a small number at the end of each row, designating the arrow set to be placed in that row.

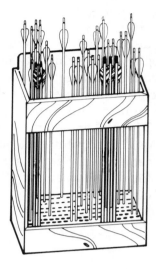

**Figure F.5** Arrows can be stored in a wooden box that separates arrows and keeps fletching from being matted down by other arrows. Students can be assigned a row for storing their arrows.

Particularly if your equipment is new, you may have to set up your equipment. The following lists necessary things to do:

1. Unless your recurve bows come with arrow rests installed, you must first install arrow rests, matching right-handed rests to right-handed bows and left-handed rests with left-handed equipment. Follow the instructions for replacing an arrow rest in Step 17, ''Maintaining Your Equipment.''

2. You should place nock locators on bowstrings. Nock locators are absolutely necessary for reasonably accurate shooting and for safe shooting. Without a nock locator, a student can vary the position of the nock end of the arrow several inches, affecting the impact point of the arrow by yards!

- To install a nock locator, place a bow square on the bowstring, with its bottom edge just resting on the arrow rest. Locate the point on the bowstring opposite the bottom edge of the bow square. From this

point, move up the width of an arrow nock plus 1/8 inch and mark the string. Install the nock locator here. Place the metal ring on the string with the bottom edge at your mark, and squeeze the ring shut with a pair of nocking pliers. Do not overtighten, because the fibers of the bowstring underneath could then eventually wear and break. Use the proper size of nock locator for the number of strands in the bowstring.

- If you do not have metal nock locators, you can make a nock locator with waxed dental floss. Cut a piece approximately 2 feet in length. Tie one end of the floss around the bowstring at your mark, cutting off the small excess end. Now wind the dental floss around the string at, and slightly above, your mark until it is large enough to prevent an arrow nock from sliding over it (see Figure F.6). Tie the floss off with a small knot and cut back the loose ends as closely as possible. This kind of nock locator will eventually fray and have to be replaced, but it is inexpensive and much better than no nock locator at all.

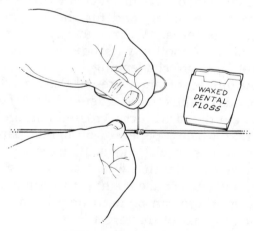

**Figure F.6** An inexpensive nock locator can be made by wrapping waxed dental floss around the bowstring.

3. Place a bow tip protector on the bottom limb tip of each bow.

4. Install bowsights (this can be delayed until Step 6). Move the sight aperture up and out of

the way or remove it until students learn to use bowsights in Step 7. If you do not have commercially made sights, make your own, following the directions in Step 6, or have students make their own sights when they come to Step 6.

5. Your shooting range must be prepared. Inspect target stands and target butts. Grass fiber butts should be wet down, if this is consistent with the manufacturer's instructions. You should also prepare any warning signs necessary and check them daily.

6. You should prepare a tackle box to take to the shooting range daily if your range is away from the equipment storage area. This can save trips back to the equipment area. This is particularly important because you cannot leave your class to shoot unsupervised. A list of items you may want to place in the box is found in Table F.3.

**Table F.3　Tackle Box Contents**

| Personal accessories | Equipment maintenance |
|---|---|
| Whistle | Adhesive tape |
| Adhesive tape | Masking tape |
| Spare finger tabs | Felt marker |
| Spare arm guards | Spare arrow rests |
| Spare clothing shields | Spare bowsight parts |
| Rubber bands and hairpins to tie hair away from bowstring | Allen wrenches (to tighten bowsights) |
| Towelettes | Spare bowstrings |
| Baby powder to dry palms | Cord bow stringer |
| Eye patch | String wax |
| Pencils | Spare nock locators |
| Scorecards | Nocking pliers |
| Golf tees to check alignment | Spare fletching |
| | Fletching cement |
| | Spare nocks |
| | Bale pins |

7. You should also have a first aid kit on the shooting range. Suggested contents for this first aid kit are given in Table F.4 and includes bandages, cleansing materials, antiseptics, and cold packs.

**Table F.4　First Aid Kit Contents**

| Injury treatment | Bandaging and cushioning |
|---|---|
| Cleansing tissues | Gauze patches |
| First aid cream | Adhesive tape |
| Antiseptic | Adhesive bandages |
| Hydrogen peroxide | Moleskin |
| Menthiolate | Safety pins |
| Neosporin | Eye patches |
| Cotton balls | |
| Cold packs | |
| Insect repellent | |

## SAFETY

Safety is an ongoing concern in archery. Safety rules and procedures are discussed in depth in Step 2. Here are several concerns that need immediate attention:

1. The security of the shooting range is your responsibility. You must prepare and post warning signs sufficient to keep pedestrians from walking onto the range. If you are indoors, you should post signs even on locked doors; many staff have keys to those doors! You may decide that some areas should be roped off, such as a sidewalk behind the shooting range. Make secure an area at least 20 yards wide on either side of your shooting range and at least 40 yards behind it.

2. When conducting your classes, check for pedestrians walking onto the range despite your warning signs, before you give the signal to begin shooting.

3. Insist that your students always straddle the shooting line. In general, have everyone shoot from the same line. If it is desirable to have students shoot at varying distances and you have portable target butts, move the target butts, thus varying the distance to targets while all archers stay on the same shooting line.

4. From the first time students have access to equipment, including during fitting of equipment, remind them not to draw and release the bow without an arrow in it, and not to point an arrow either in or out of the bow at anyone.

## PRECLASS CHECKLIST

There are many things to check upon and organize before each class. Here is a suggested list of things to do before class. You may add to this as necessary for your facilities.

- Secure the shooting range by posting signs, locking doors or gates, or inspecting permanent signs as necessary.
- Prepare target faces. You may even want to post them before class.
- Have any scorecards necessary ready with clipboards and pencils.
- Have special equipment needed for the day, such as balloons or video cameras, ready.
- Open the equipment cabinet or storage area.
- Have your tackle box and first aid kit ready.

## LIABILITY CHECKLIST

The reminders below address your legal responsibility for seeing that your archery class is as safe as possible:

- Post rules where they can be seen every day (at the shooting range or equipment cabinet where students obtain their equipment).
- Provide adequate supervision. Never leave your class shooting unsupervised.
- Provide proper first aid and plan possible emergency medical treatment. Develop a plan of action that can be executed immediately in case of accident. Failure to do so can result in your being negligent.

- Provide safe equipment. You must regularly and thoroughly inspect all equipment provided students. Repair defective equipment or remove it from use.
- Provide a safe environment. You are expected to post the appropriate warning signs and check on them daily. You must also monitor the range during shooting to quickly detect the presence of individuals ignoring warning signs.
- Warn students of the inherent risks of archery and encourage them to ask questions. You have a duty not only to inform your students but to be sure they understand.
- Shoot from reasonable distances to reasonably sized targets. Novice archers should not shoot long distances or at small targets because a few experienced archers are in the same class.
- Be knowledgeable of insurance coverage. Take steps to protect yourself. Keep records, particularly those involving accidents, for at least five years.
- Plan your course soundly. Use progressions, such as mimicking without equipment, mimicking with equipment, then shooting arrows.
- Evaluate your students' mental and physical fitness. Assess any injuries or physical handicaps in order to identify if such disabilities limit safe participation. Ascertain the mental attitudes of students, keeping in mind that a bow can be a lethal weapon.
- Remember that your students have civil rights, and you are not entitled to violate them, even in an educational setting.

# *Step 1* Fitting Basic Equipment

Fitting archery equipment to the shooter properly is important for two reasons—safety and enjoyment. Several aspects of fitting minimize the risks of injury. First, arrows of the proper length minimize the danger of overdrawing. Second, a bow of proper draw weight can be held long enough to steady and aim the shot more accurately. Finally, accessories such as an arm guard and a finger tab prevent blisters and soreness. Furthermore, any archer shoots properly-fitted equipment more accurately than ill-fitted equipment. When shooting is more accurate, the archer experiences a greater sense of accomplishment and enjoys the sport more.

Fitting a large group of students is difficult because individuals of varying size, strength, and handedness can comprise your groups from semester to semester. Fortunately, beginning archers do not need perfect fits. There is a range of equipment that is safe for them to use, and allows reasonable progress as they learn basic shooting technique. Therefore, as instructor, you must exercise good judgment in giving each student the best available fit, but considering that the entire group must be outfitted with equipment.

This step outlines the procedure to follow in fitting archery equipment to a class of students. The sequence is the same as that outlined in *Archery: Steps to Success*, but in several cases methods better suited for fitting a large group of shooters in the shortest possible time are substituted for the methods in the participant's book. A master sheet for recording all pertinent information for the entire class is provided in this step (see Table 1.1). You may want to post a copy of this sheet near the equipment cabinet so that students can refer to it if they forget their equipment assignments.

## CONDUCTING EQUIPMENT FITTING EFFICIENTLY

Assigning equipment to a large group of students is time consuming. The methods suggested here should save as much time as possible. At the first class, eye dominance, draw length, and whether the student should shoot right- or left-handed must be determined. Accessories can be selected by some students while you are determining the draw lengths of others. However, you can make bow-and-arrow set assignments on your own before the next class and post these assignments for the students. This may allow you the time to address safety at the first class and perhaps introduce mimicking as well.

## STRINGING BOWS

Modern recurve bows can be left strung during the several months of a year that you teach archery. Leaving the bows strung saves the time required for students to string and unstring them every day, allowing more shooting time. Students should be taught how to string a bow, but you can choose when best to introduce this topic.

However, you may have to unstring bows every day if you do not have sufficient space to store them strung. In this event, students must be taught the proper and safe methods of stringing at the first or second class meeting. If you have a box or wall stringer, you obviously should teach students those methods of stringing and unstringing their bows. If students stagger their arrival at class some can have their bows strung before others arrive and a bottleneck at the stringer can be avoided. If you have a large class or all students arrive at one time, however, you may

Table 1.1  Equipment Assignments

Class meeting days _____   Time _____   Section number _____   Semester _____

| | Student name | Eye dominance | Shoots R or L? | Draw length | Bow length[a] | Bow weight[b] | Bow # assigned | Adjusted weight | Arrow length[c] | Shaft size | Arrows assigned | Tab # | Arm guard # |
|---|---|---|---|---|---|---|---|---|---|---|---|---|---|
| 1 | | | | | | | | | | | | | |
| 2 | | | | | | | | | | | | | |
| 3 | | | | | | | | | | | | | |
| 4 | | | | | | | | | | | | | |
| 5 | | | | | | | | | | | | | |
| 6 | | | | | | | | | | | | | |
| 7 | | | | | | | | | | | | | |
| 8 | | | | | | | | | | | | | |
| 9 | | | | | | | | | | | | | |
| 10 | | | | | | | | | | | | | |
| 11 | | | | | | | | | | | | | |
| 12 | | | | | | | | | | | | | |
| 13 | | | | | | | | | | | | | |
| 14 | | | | | | | | | | | | | |
| 15 | | | | | | | | | | | | | |
| 16 | | | | | | | | | | | | | |
| 17 | | | | | | | | | | | | | |
| 18 | | | | | | | | | | | | | |
| 19 | | | | | | | | | | | | | |
| 20 | | | | | | | | | | | | | |
| 21 | | | | | | | | | | | | | |
| 22 | | | | | | | | | | | | | |
| 23 | | | | | | | | | | | | | |
| 24 | | | | | | | | | | | | | |

[a] Bow length assigned according to draw lengths: under 24 in., 60–64 in.; 25–26 in., 65–66 in.; 27–28 in., 67–68 in.; over 29 in., 69–70 in.

[b] Youth: 15–20 lb.; adult: 20–25 lb.; strong adult: 25–30 lb.

[c] Add 3.75 in. to draw length.

want to have a number of cord stringers available. They are inexpensive, and the time required for stringing and unstringing can be minimized when several students can string at once. If you do not have a box or wall stringer, cord stringers are the method of choice.

Students should learn the step-through method of stringing a bow. Recall that this method must be used properly to reduce the chance of gradually damaging a bow by repetitiously twisting its limbs each time it is strung. Teaching the proper method is helpful for students who may choose this method of stringing personal equipment in the future.

However, you may stress the disadvantages of this method in comparison to using a cord stringer.

Be sure to stress the safety aspects of stringing that are covered in the discussion of stringing methods in Step 1 of *Archery: Steps to Success*, regardless of which methods you introduce. It is important that the student keep the head and eyes out of the way, in case the bow should slip as it is being strung or unstrung. Every student should also get into the habit of checking that the bowstring is properly seated in the limb notch before walking away to the shooting range with the bow.

Box bowstringer method

Step-through method

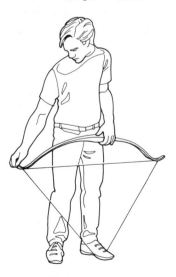

Cord bowstringer method

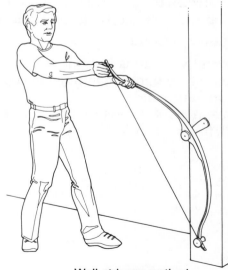

Wall stringer method

# Fitting Procedure

## *1. Eye Dominance*
[Corresponds to *Archery*, Step 1, Exercise 1]

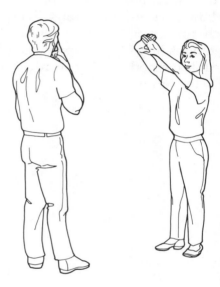

### Group Management and Safety Tips

- Students should line up or sit on the floor so that each has a clear view of your face.
- Show students how to form a small opening between the skin webs (between the thumb and forefinger) of their two hands.

### Instructions to Class

- "Extend your arms in front of you."
- "Look at my right eye through the opening in your hands."
- "Take note of whether I say 'right eye' or 'left eye' to you."

### Instructor Activity

- Go to each student one by one.
- The eye you see through the opening in the student's hands is the dominant eye.
- Tell each student which eye you see.
- Record each student's dominant eye.

## 2. *Determining Handedness for Shooting*
[New drill]

### Group Management and Safety Tips

- Students who are right-handed and right-eye dominant should shoot right-handed.
- Students who are left-handed and left-eye dominant should shoot left-handed.
- A student who is mixed dominant should decide between two alternatives:
  a. Shoot on the side of the dominant eye (opposite handedness).
  b. Close the dominant eye when shooting, aiming with the eye on the same side of the body as the draw hand. If a student prefers this method but has trouble closing the dominant eye, even after a little practice, he or she can patch the dominant eye. A convenient way to do this is by taping over that lens of an inexpensive pair of sunglasses and removing the lens of the aiming eye.
- Record whether each student will shoot right-handed or left-handed.

## 3. *Determining Draw Length*
[Corresponds to *Archery*, Step 1, Exercise 2]

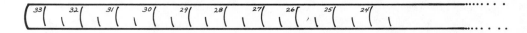

### Equipment Needed

- 1 light-poundage right-hand bow and 1 light-poundage left-hand bow
- 1 measuring arrow. You can make a measuring arrow from the longest arrow shaft you can obtain. It need not have a point or fletching, but it should have a nock. Place a yardstick along the side of the arrow shaft, the stick's zero end positioned at the base of the slit in the nock. Starting at 24 inches, mark every half-inch to the end of the arrow shaft with a permanent felt marker. Number the full-inch marks 24, 25, and so on as appropriate.

### Group Management and Safety Tips

- Have your students sit or stand where they can see you.
- Taking a bow, demonstrate to the class.
- Show them how to hold the bow and place the first three fingers of their right or left hands (depending on whether they are shooting right- or left-handed) around the middle of the bowstring. Demonstrate raising the bow arm and drawing the hand back under the chin, with the string touching the middle of the chin and nose. Now have students mimic the draw.
- One by one, have your students take the appropriate (right or left) light-poundage bow and practice drawing several times. Help each one nock the measuring arrow and draw back, as you note the number on the arrow shaft just at, or in front of, the arrow rest. When measuring, students should direct the measuring arrow toward a target butt. Instruct students to ease the bowstring back to the relaxed position when you have noted the draw length.
- The first student who completes this measurement can assist you by recording the draw length of each following student.

As students later refine their technique and perhaps choose to use a different anchor point, you may want to remeasure their draw length and fit their equipment more precisely.

## 4. Determining Ideal Bow Length

[Corresponds to *Archery*, Step 1, Exercise 3]

*Note.* If all of your class bows are the same length, skip this drill.

**Group Management and Safety Tips**

- Using the key on the bottom of your master sheet (see Table 1.1), determine the ideal bow length for each student from his or her draw length.

## 5. Determining Bow Weight

[Corresponds to *Archery*, Step 1, Exercise 4]

**Group Management and Safety Tips**

- Assigning a bow weight to a student is a subjective judgment on your part as instructor. Consider the individual's size and apparent strength.
- Generally, young people shoot with bows 15–20 pounds in draw weight, adults shoot bows 20–25 pounds in draw weight, and stronger adults shoot bows 25–30 pounds in draw weight.
- Consider the archer's draw length. You can estimate the draw weight your student will actually shoot by subtracting or adding 2 pounds for every inch the draw length is less than or more than, respectively, the standard at which the bow draw weight was measured by the manufacturer. Older bows were measured at a draw length of 28 inches from the back of the bow, newer bows at a draw length of 26 1/4 inches from the arrow rest. A column for estimated draw weight is provided on the class chart.
- It is better to give a beginner a bow that is too light than one that is too heavy. An archer can always use a heavier bow later, but if a heavy bow leads a beginner to develop poor technique, it will be difficult for the archer to overcome bad habits.

# 6. *Fitting the Best Arrow*
[Corresponds to *Archery*, Step 1, Exercise 5]

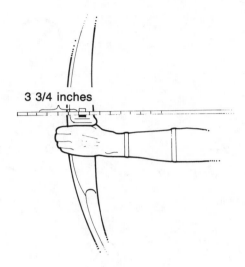

3 3/4 inches

## Group Management and Safety Tips

• To determine the arrow length for a beginner, simply add 3 3/4 inches to the archer's draw length. This provides the archer with a long arrow, minimizing the chances of overdrawing. Once an archer has perfected his or her form, you may want to refit him or her with arrows that are only 1–2 inches longer than the draw length. This usually gives better arrow flight and less arrow weight for shooting longer distances.

• To determine the proper shaft size, consult Table 1.2 in *Archery: Steps to Success* if you are using fiberglass shafts or Table 16.1 if you are using aluminum shafts. You need the adjusted draw weight and arrow length for each student. However, you are fitting beginning students with very long arrows as a safety precaution at this time; the shaft size designated by the tables will probably result in a rather big, heavy arrow for most students. It is recommended that you base arrow shaft size on a length only 2 inches longer than the draw length.

## 7. *Fitting Accessories*
[Corresponds to *Archery*, Step 1, Exercise 6]

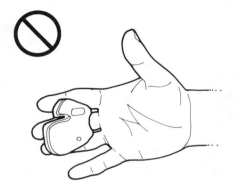

Finger tab is too small.

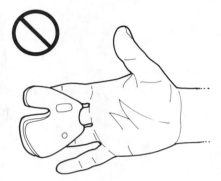

Finger tab is too large.

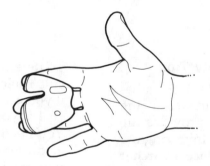

A correctly sized finger tab.

### Group Management and Safety Tips

- Demonstrate how an arm guard and a finger tab are worn.
- Demonstrate a proper finger tab size—one that would cover the fingers but not have excess material.
- Place right- and left-handed finger tabs in separate containers so that students do not choose the wrong tab.
- Have students pick up their accessories when they are finished fitting their draw lengths.
- Remind students to record the numbers on their arm guards and finger tabs.
- Have students pick up any other accessories, such as quivers, that you want them to have.

# *Step 2*  Shooting With Safety in Mind

Archery can be taught as safely as any other activity. However, everyone involved must keep in mind that safety comes from following certain rules and procedures to the smallest detail. Instructor and student alike must respect the fact that a bow and arrow can be a lethal weapon in the hands of someone who ignores safety or is careless.

In the introduction to this text, we reviewed the safety procedures you should follow in planning and conducting your classes on a daily basis. However, safety is necessarily a responsibility you share with your students. Students should be taught safety also so that any experiences they have with archery outside a class are safe ones. In this step, we discuss the safety material that you should review with your students BEFORE they shoot. We also discuss the manner in which students demonstrate that they know and understand this material.

## DISCUSSING DANGERS AND SAFETY RULES

A list of safety rules is presented in Step 2 of *Archery: Steps to Success*. Although you should instruct your students to read and study these rules, it is your responsibility also to review these rules in class and discuss the dangers associated with ignoring the rules, as well as discuss the inherent dangers of archery. You should also give your students an opportunity to ask questions about any of these topics.

You may want to obtain a signed statement of informed consent following this safety discussion. Although some students—particularly those who are minors—may not be able to waive their rights, such a signed statement demonstrates that you, the instructor, took every reasonable step to make your students aware of the risks. A suggested written form is included in Table 2.1. You can change or adapt it as you wish. If you use such a form, you may want to keep a copy for yourself and provide each student with another copy to which he or she can refer.

The suggested topics for your safety discussion follow:

*1. Safety Rules:* Review the safety rules presented in Step 2 of *Archery: Steps to Success*. You may need to add additional rules to accommodate your shooting range and specific situation.

*2. Inherent Risks:* The inherent risks in archery arise from equipment and from classmates or peers ignoring or carelessly overlooking safety rules. Equipment can fail even if it is maintained properly and inspected frequently. You should stress to the students that they should participate daily in the inspection procedure and report anything suspicious in the condition of their equipment. This minimizes their risk due to equipment failure.

**Table 2.1   Warning for Archery**

Archery is a reasonably safe sport as long as certain rules are obeyed.

Archery requires upper body strength and muscle endurance. When you use proper technique, much of the work is done by your back muscles. If you have any physical condition that precludes you from an activity of this type, such as a back or neck injury, please obtain a physician's consent to participate.

There is a slight possibility that an injury can occur in archery due to the failure of equipment. However, you will be given time to inspect your equipment every day, and doing so will minimize the risk of equipment failure's causing injury. Call to your instructor's attention (a) any crack in or other damage to your bow; (b) any fraying, cut, or unraveling of your bowstring; (c) any crack or splinter in your arrows, or a loose tip or nock; and (d) any suspicious condition in your equipment.

There is a possibility that injury can occur in archery if you or your classmates do not obey safety rules or are careless. Do your part by obeying each and every rule to the smallest detail and by reporting to your instructor any violations of safety rules by your classmates.

You will have access to a complete list of safety rules and will be required to demonstrate your knowledge of these rules. Among these rules are the warnings to

- never point an arrow, particularly one in a bow, toward anyone
- never shoot an arrow high into the air
- never shoot at a target when someone is in the vicinity of the target, or even could be in the vicinity, unseen by you
- approach arrows in the target carefully and pull them from the target only after checking that the area behind you is clear
- use only the equipment fitted for you and assigned to you
- never draw past your anchor point
- wait for signals from your instructor or a person your instructor designates before beginning shooting or retrieving arrows

If you have any questions, direct them to your instructor.

I have read the preceding and certify that I am physically fit for archery. I further attest I will read, study, and follow the archery rules made available to me. I have read and understand the information above. I fully know, understand, and appreciate the risks inherent in archery. I am voluntarily participating in this activity.

_____ Age _____ Date _____
(Signature)

USE OF PERSONAL EQUIPMENT

If I provide my own equipment, I understand that I am responsible for its safety and good operating condition, regardless of where I obtain it.

_____ Date _____
(Signature)

Students must be made aware that each and every one of them has a role in making the class safe for everyone. Students must do their individual parts by obeying safety rules to the smallest detail. They should not overlook the safety violations of their classmates, because they could be putting themselves as well as other students at greater risk. Such violations should be reported to you if a nicely presented reminder goes unregarded.

**3. Dangers of Improper Equipment Usage:** Students must appreciate how dangerous archery equipment can be. Point out to them that arrow tips are sharp and can inflict an injury if not handled properly, even without the arrow being loaded in a bow (see Figure 2.1).

The nock end of an arrow also can cause an eye injury.

Loaded into a bow, the arrow has more potential for injury because of the thrust provided by the bow (see Figure 2.2). Drawing a bowstring back even an inch and releasing it can cause an arrow to fly many yards. It may help students to know that a shot arrow can penetrate some materials more easily than a bullet from a handgun. With this knowledge, students should appreciate your reminders that an arrow should be shot only to a target and only when the target area is clear of other archers, spectators, or passersby. An arrow should never be shot into the air, a wooded area, or any other place that the archer cannot see is absolutely clear of people.

**Figure 2.1** Arrows should be carried with the tips held in the palm of the hand.

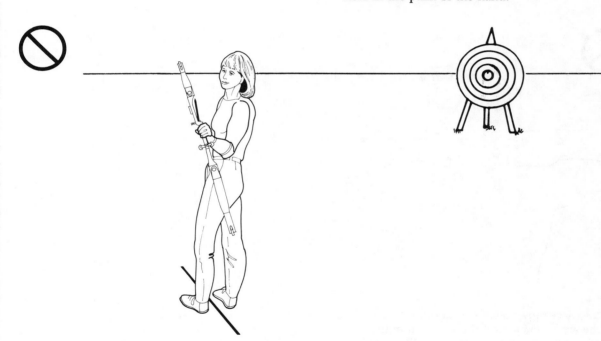

**Figure 2.2** Beginners often unknowingly point a loaded bow at someone if they turn to talk to a classmate while standing on the shooting line.

Archery equipment is designed to be used in a specific way. Warn students that using it in any other way may cause an injury that cannot be easily foreseen. Improper usage can also damage equipment, making it dangerous at a later time, even with proper usage.

**4. Dangers of Improper Techniques:** Stress to students that you will teach them to shoot properly and safely. Their varying from the technique being taught to them can have dangers they cannot easily predict. Stress particularly that the archer always places the arrow on the bowstring against the nock locator. Placing it much higher or lower would send the arrow off in an extreme direction. Overdrawing can be dangerous because an arrow drawn off the arrow rest can lodge in the archer's arm if the string is released—or in the bow, causing the arrow to break. If the broken arrow is wood or fiberglass, a splinter can lodge in the bow arm; if it is aluminum, a jagged edge could cut the skin. An overdrawn string can also hook behind the shooter's ear (see Figure 2.3).

Be sure to give thorough and honest answers to any questions students may have on archery safety and the risks and dangers of shooting.

## DEMONSTRATING SAFETY KNOWLEDGE

Students should demonstrate their knowledge of the archery safety rules in Step 2 of *Archery: Steps to Success* before they are permitted to shoot. A suggested test on these rules is included in this step. Students who do not score well should be required to take the test again. Even students who score well should be allowed to review any items missed and the safety rules pertinent to those items.

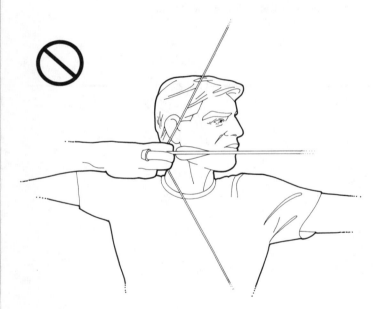

**Figure 2.3** A beginner often overdraws the bow, risking the arrow coming off the back end of the arrow rest or catching the bowstring on the face.

## SAFETY TEST

Name _____ Class _____ Date _____ Score _____

**Multiple Choice Questions**

*Directions*: Place the letter of the *best* answer on the line to the left of the question.

_____ 1. Which is the proper way to stand at the shooting line?
    a. Place both feet behind the line
    b. Place both feet on the line
    c. Straddle the line
    d. Place the rear foot on the line

_____ 2. Which of the following is *not* proper procedure for nocking an arrow?
    a. You may nock an arrow once you are on the shooting line
    b. You should nock the arrow only at the nock locator
    c. You should point a nocked arrow only at the ground or target
    d. You should nock an arrow after the signal to shoot

_____ 3. Which of the following is the emergency signal to stop shooting?
    a. A verbal "stop" signal
    b. One blast on a whistle
    c. Two blasts on a whistle
    d. Three or more blasts on a whistle

_____ 4. If your arrow falls off the arrow rest while you are drawing, what should you do?
    a. Start your shot over
    b. Hold the arrow in place with your forefinger
    c. Squeeze the nock with your draw hand and swing the arrow back into place
    d. Release the bowstring

_____ 5. When is it permissible to shoot an arrow straight up?
    a. After checking to see that the area is clear
    b. After one whistle blast
    c. When testing a bow for distance
    d. Never

_____ 6. What should you do when you finish shooting your arrows?
    a. Stand on the line until the whistle blows
    b. Ask the person next to you whether you may move back
    c. Step back from the shooting line
    d. Tell your instructor that you are finished

_____ 7. When should you retrieve arrows that fall short of the target?
    a. After scoring the arrows in the target
    b. On the walk to the target
    c. On the walk back to the shooting line
    d. At the end of class

_____ 8. Which of the following is *not* an appropriate step in pulling arrows from the target?
    a. Check to be sure no one is in the way
    b. Put one hand flat against the target face near the arrow
    c. Grab the arrow nock and pull
    d. Twist the arrow back and forth while pulling

**Short Answer Questions**

*Directions*: Fill in the blank or provide a short answer as required.

9. List two inspections to make on your bowstring before shooting.

   a. Inspect the _____ for _____

   b. Inspect the _____ for _____

10. List two inspections to make on a recurve bow before shooting.

   a. Inspect the _____ for _____

   b. Inspect the _____ for _____

11. List three inspections to make on each arrow before shooting.

   a. Inspect the _____ for _____

   b. Inspect the _____ for _____

   c. Inspect the _____ for _____

12. Name two items that you should *not* wear when shooting archery.

   a. _____

   b. _____

13. Name three items that you *should* wear when shooting archery.

   a. _____

   b. _____

   c. _____

14. Why should archers *not* run to the target?


15. What two ways can you use to carry arrows?

**Safety Test Answers**

1. c
2. a
3. d
4. a
5. d
6. c
7. b
8. c
9. a. bowstring for fraying or broken strands
   b. serving for unraveling
10. a. limbs for cracks
    b. brace height for minimum height of 6 inches
11. a. shafts for cracks
    b. tips for proper installation
    c. nocks for cracks
12. a. baggy shirts and sleeves
    b. chest pockets with buttons
    c. chest pockets with pens or pencils
    d. necklaces and pins
13. a. shoes
    b. arm guard
    c. finger tab
    d. hair band
14. may trip and fall into arrow nocks, injuring an eye
15. in a quiver or with the points in the palm of hand

# *Step 3*   Mimicking Basic Form

Novice archers display a variety of skill levels, even when only mimicking the basic archery shot. Develop a critical eye for identifying performance differences. Correcting a new archer's flaws now will make the first few shots with an arrow more successful and safe.

Four components of the mimicked shot are listed below, with characteristics of archers at three skill levels—beginning, intermediate, and advanced. You can use these descriptors as an observation guide or as an evaluation tool. You can also use the descriptors in the ''Keys to Success'' (located in the participant's book). With practice, you will soon be able to differentiate the three skill levels.

## *Mimicking Basic Form Rating*

| CRITERION | BEGINNING LEVEL | INTERMEDIATE LEVEL | ADVANCED LEVEL |
|---|---|---|---|
| **Stance** | • Takes a different stance for each shot, ignoring shooting line<br><br>• Turns upper body to face target<br><br>• Has weight on front or rear foot | • Places feet too close together or too far apart<br><br>• Stands with toes even but not along a line to bull's-eye | • Consistently takes a stance with toes along a line to bull's-eye<br>• Distributes weight evenly |
| **Draw Hand Hook** | • Forms fist with draw hand<br><br>• Hooks onto string with all four fingers | • Uses three fingers, but curls fingers | • Forms three-finger hook and keeps back of hand flat<br>• Has a relaxed draw hand |

## Mimicking Basic Form Rating

| CRITERION | BEGINNING LEVEL | INTERMEDIATE LEVEL | ADVANCED LEVEL |
|---|---|---|---|
| **Draw** | • Draws with draw elbow pointed downward<br><br>• Draws using arm muscles by first bending draw elbow<br>• Bends bow arm elbow<br><br><br>• Bends bow arm wrist in or out<br>• Has bow arm in path of string | • Uses back muscles and arm muscles, making draw arm oblique<br>• Executes a jerky or slow draw<br><br>• Lets bow shoulder elevate<br><br>• Cants bow | • Initiates draw by moving elbow back with back muscles<br>• Relaxes the draw arm<br><br>• Brings draw arm back along a line to the target<br>• Draws smoothly and quickly<br>• Holds bow vertically<br>• Rotates bow elbow |
| **Anchor** | • Draws past anchor position<br><br>• Stops before reaching anchor position<br>• Draws to chest level | • Touches string with chin or nose, but not both<br><br>• Lets draw hand float below chin | • Anchors with middle of chin and nose both touching string<br>• Anchors with draw hand in contact with jaw |

# Error Detection and Correction for Mimicking Basic Form

As you observe your students, you will find that certain errors typically occur. Look for the following errors in particular. Some apply to mimicking both with and without a bow; others apply only to mimicking with a bow. If you find one of these errors, refer to the right-hand side of the page to find out how to correct it. Select one error at a time to correct. It is generally best to correct errors affecting T-alignment first.

Your students' mimicking provides an opportunity for you to observe them from the back, the sides, and the front. Move around to observe archers from various angles, but especially take advantage of standing in front of them, downrange, to observe their alignment with the target.

**ERROR**

**CORRECTION**

### With or Without a Bow

1. Archer shuffles stance or rotates upper body to face target.

1. Begin by aligning the archer's stance for him or her, then stress his or her standing sideways to target, simply turning the head to look at the target.

2. Archer initiates draw by flexing at elbow (the upper draw arm would then be flexed on a horizontal plane at full draw).

   *Variation*: The archer achieves the draw by elbow flexion with the elbow pointed downward.

2. This error is more likely to occur when the archer rotates the upper body to face the target. Stress that the draw is started by moving the elbow back.

   Lift the archer's elbow to shoulder level. On the next shot, remind the archer to move the elbow back at shoulder level.

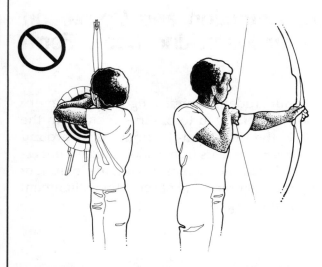

**ERROR**

**CORRECTION**

3. Archer flexes bow elbow.

3. Emphasize extending the bow arm straight to the target (''push the bow away''), then rotating the straight elbow down.

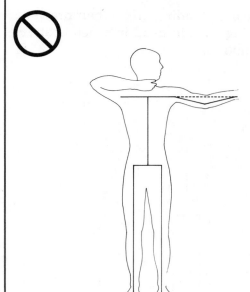

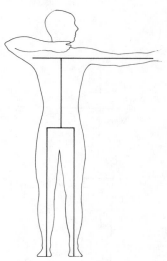

4. Archer draws past anchor position.

4. The archer should draw the string straight back, close to the bow arm, bringing draw hand under chin until the string touches chin and nose.

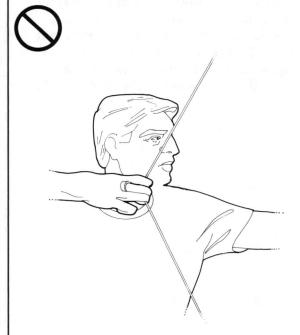

**ERROR**

**CORRECTION**

### With a Bow

5. Archer moves head to meet string.

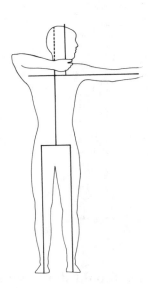

5. Emphasize standing erect, then drawing string back to head in a deliberate, fluid motion.

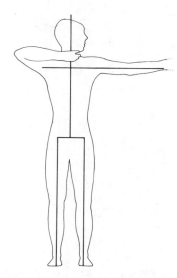

6. Archer wraps fingers around string or flexes base knuckles, perhaps putting thumb on string.

6. Show archer how to form the draw hand hook. Remind archer that it is the same position used to carry a suitcase. Emphasize that when the hand hooks onto the string, the pulling is now done by moving the elbow back.

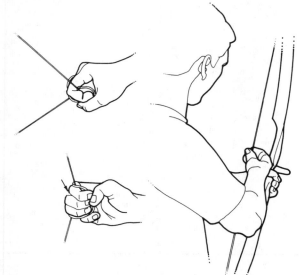

# Selected Mimicking Drills

## 1. Bow Arm Drill
[Corresponds to *Archery*, Step 3, Drill 1]

### Group Management and Safety Tips

- Have students pair up and alternate bow arm movement in this drill.

### Equipment

- None

### Instructions to Class

- "Face your partner, an arm's length away."
- "One of you should turn sideways and extend your bow arm, letting your partner put pressure on the heel of your hand."
- "Rotate your arm down and out, keeping your bow shoulder down."
- "Check your position by bending at the elbow. Your hand should come to chest level."

### Student Option

- "Do this drill individually against a door jamb."

### Student Keys to Success

- Raise bow arm to target
- Rotate elbow down

### Student Success Goal

- 10 repetitions using proper position as demonstrated by the bent arm check

### To Reduce Difficulty

- Student should hold bow arm out, palm down. Keeping arm in place, archer rotates hand at wrist to vertical position. This is the proper bow arm position.

### To Increase Difficulty

- Have your student rotate the bow arm down and out without resistance.

## 2. *Shadow Drill*
[Corresponds to *Archery*, Step 3, Drill 2]

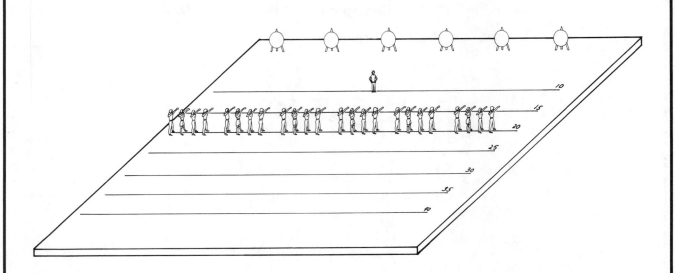

### Group Management and Safety Tips

- Have students take a position straddling a "shooting line" so that you can scan the class.
- Selectively watch students for correct execution of a mimicked shot, especially from the front and side.

### Equipment

- None

### Instructions to Class

- "Assume your stance."
- "Imagine you have a bow in your hand."
- "Draw the 'string' back to your anchor position."

### Student Options

- "Repeat in front of a mirror."
- "Repeat with eyes closed."

### Student Keys to Success

- Weight even
- Shoulders square
- Look over front shoulder
- Raise bow arm toward target
- Draw elbow back at shoulder level
- Chin on hand

### Student Success Goals

- 10 repetitions following Keys to Success, eyes open
- 10 repetitions following Keys to Success, eyes closed

### To Reduce Difficulty

- Drill is already in its simplest form.

### To Increase Difficulty

- If students can mimic the shot with good form, proceed to the following drills.

# 3. Mimicking Drill

[Corresponds to *Archery*, Step 3, Drill 3]

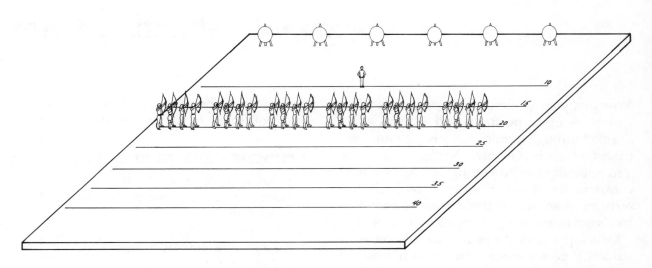

### Group Management and Safety Tips

- Designate a line on the floor as the "shooting line."
- Have students take a position straddling the line, with their bow arm sides facing you.
- Selectively watch students for correct execution of a mimicked shot, especially checking for rotation of the bow arm down and out.
- Caution students to ease bowstring back slowly, rather than release string, after anchoring and pausing.

### Equipment

- 1 bow for each student
- 1 finger tab for each student

### Instructions to Class

- "Take a stance."
- "Draw your bow to the proper anchor position."
- "Hold; then ease the string back."

### Student Options

- "Repeat in front of a mirror."
- "Repeat with eyes closed."

### Student Keys to Success

- Feet aligned
- Bow in front
- Set bow hand with bow in V of thumb and index finger
- Set draw hand hook
- Raise bow toward target
- Rotate bow elbow down
- Draw elbow back at shoulder level
- Chin on hand
- String on chin and nose

### Student Success Goals

- 10 repetitions as described in Keys to Success, eyes open
- 10 repetitions as described in Keys to Success, eyes closed

### To Reduce Difficulty

- Let student mimic the shot with the lightest poundage bow available.

### To Increase Difficulty

- Have your student mimic the shot with an arrow but without shooting. Archer should point the arrow toward a target butt; you should stand behind the shooting line. [Corresponds to *Archery*, Step 3, Drill 4]

# *Step 4*  Shooting Form

Now that your students have become familiar with some of the positions and movements in the shot through mimicking, it is time for them to shoot their first arrows. Nocking the arrow and releasing the bowstring are the two new components of shooting an arrow. Characteristics of archers at the three different skill levels are listed in the rating table that follows.

Develop a critical eye for identifying your students' performance differences in nocking and releasing, but remember to check for the characteristics of shooting form you examined in their mimicking, too. Even if an archer correctly executed these components of shooting while only mimicking, the greater attention now given to the arrow can lead the archer to overlook those fundamental components.

## STUDENT KEYS TO SUCCESS

- Stand using good posture
- Nock arrow against nock indicator
- Set bow hand
- Set draw hand hook
- Raise bow toward target
- Relax hands
- Draw elbow back
- Anchor
- Concentrate on target
- Relax draw hand to release string
- Follow-through

## *Shooting Form Rating*

| CRITERION | BEGINNING LEVEL | INTERMEDIATE LEVEL | ADVANCED LEVEL |
|---|---|---|---|
| Nocking | • Nocks arrow with odd-color feather toward bow<br><br>• Sets hook with all fingers above or below arrow<br>• Fails to place arrow below and against nock locator | • Nocks arrow with odd-color feather away from bow<br><br>• Pinches nock between fingers<br><br>• Curls fingers to twist arrow off rest | • Nocks arrow with odd-color feather away from bow<br>• Sets hook without squeezing arrow nock<br>• Keeps back of hand flat |

## Shooting Form Rating

| CRITERION | BEGINNING LEVEL | INTERMEDIATE LEVEL | ADVANCED LEVEL |
|---|---|---|---|
| **Release and Follow-Through** | • Extends fingers one at a time to release<br><br>• Flings fingers open and draws hand away from head<br>or<br>• Pushes draw hand forward to release<br><br>• Grabs bow with bow hand and drops arm on release<br>• Lets bow arm bend at elbow | • Dead release: Opens fingers with hand locked into position<br>• Torques bow by grabbing it<br><br><br>• Moves head to watch arrow fly | • Relaxes fingers to release<br><br>• Lets back tension carry hand back over rear shoulder<br><br>• Keeps bow arm up and bow hand relaxed<br>• Maintains head position |

# Error Detection and Correction for Shooting Form

As novice archers shoot their first arrows, there are errors that tend to occur. The more quickly they are corrected, the more rewarding shooting will be for the archers. Look for the following errors, correcting them one at a time. It is best to correct those related to T-alignment first because poor alignment can predispose an archer to other mistakes. You have to observe from the side or back, now that the archers are shooting arrows. Take care to sight down a straight line to the target from behind the archer in order to check for alignment.

**ERROR**

**CORRECTION**

1. Archer cannot keep arrow on arrow rest throughout draw.

1. The archer is probably flexing the draw fingers or hand, or pinching the arrow nock between the fingers. Emphasize that the hand merely hooks onto the string, with the back muscles doing the work of the draw, and the wrist and base knuckles stay relaxed.

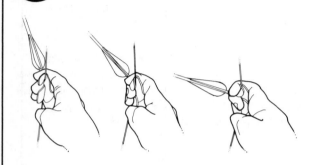

2. String strikes bow arm.

2. Be sure the archer is rotating the bow arm down and out. Also, the bow wrist must be straight, not hyperextended. If the archer's bow arm structure is such that this is still a problem, open the stance slightly and/or give the archer a long-style arm guard.

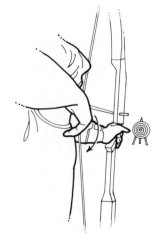

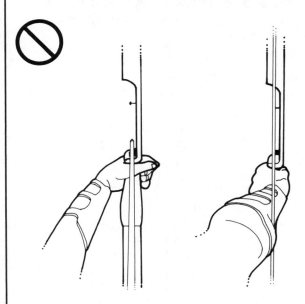

3. Archer holds bow with flexed or hyperextended wrist.

3. Have the archer visualize a line running down the center of the arm. This line should meet the center of the bow handle.

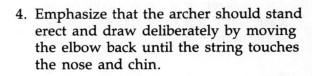

4. Archer shifts weight to front foot and leans toward target.

4. Emphasize that the archer should stand erect and draw deliberately by moving the elbow back until the string touches the nose and chin.

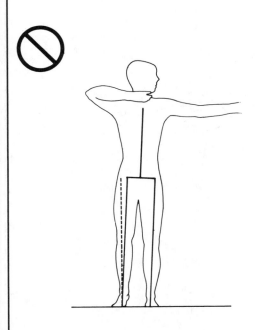

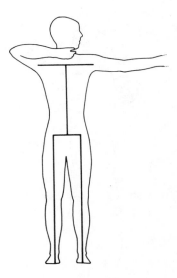

**ERROR**

**CORRECTION**

5. Archer leans away from target, allowing front shoulder to elevate.

5. Make sure the archer does not have too heavy a bow. Then emphasize that the archer stands straight and draws deliberately by moving the elbow back.

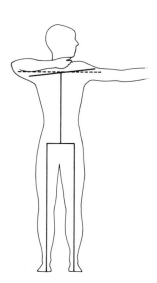
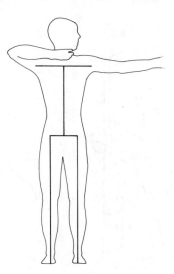

6. Archer extends at draw elbow on release and flings the hand out, away from the face.

6. Cue the archer to increase back tension during aiming and to release by relaxing the hand to simply not hold the string any longer.

**ERROR**                     **CORRECTION**

7. Archer extends fingers in succession in order to release.

7. Have the archer practice mimicking the release by relaxing the hand, rather than by forcing the release.

8. Archer moves head and drops bow arm to watch arrow.

8. Emphasize maintaining visual focus on the bull's-eye until hearing the arrow hit the target.

# Selected Shooting Form Drills

## 1. Partner Check Drill
[Corresponds to *Archery*, Step 4, Drill 1]

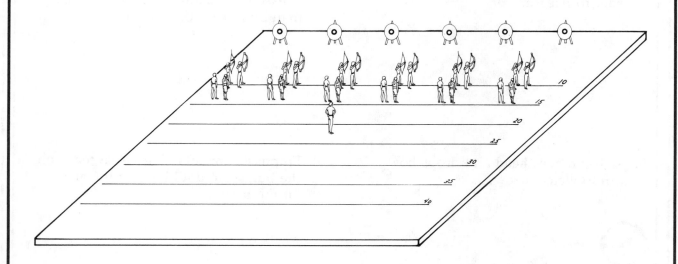

### Group Management and Safety Tips

- Assign four students to a target butt. Have them hang a 12-inch paper plate in the middle of their target butt.
- Have students pair up; they will shoot alternately and observe each other.
- Class should shoot from the 10-yard line.
- Remind observers to stay behind archers.
- Individually observe students to provide help and clue observers.

### Equipment

- Bow, finger tab, arm guard, 6 arrows, and quiver for each student
- 1 target butt, a 12-inch paper plate for every four students (two pairs of partners)
- 2 bale pins for every target butt

### Instructions to Class

- ''Shooting partner, first take 1 shot to let observing partner watch your form.''
- ''Take 5 more shots. Observers, try to catch your shooting partner varying form.''
- ''Observing partners, tell your shooter to let down if the bow arm is in the path of the bowstring.''

### Student Option

- ''Shoot without an observer, trying to establish the same feel on all shots.'' [Corresponds to *Archery*, Step 4, Drill 2]

### Student Success Goals

- 3 shots with identical form out of 5 attempts, on 2 successive ends
- Shoot-alone option: 12 repetitions as described in the Keys to Success

### To Reduce Difficulty

- Drill is already in its easiest form.

### To Increase Difficulty

- You could change the Success Goal to 5 shots with identical form out of 5 attempts.
- Have your student shoot 6 ends.

## 2.  *Scoring Drill*

[Corresponds to *Archery*, Step 4, Drill 3]

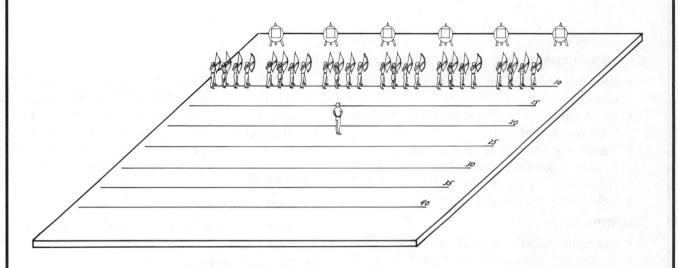

### Group Management and Safety Tips

- Assign three or four students to each target.
- Students shoot 6-arrow ends from a 10-yard shooting line.
- Selectively watch shooters.

### Equipment

- Shooting tackle and 6 arrows for each student
- 1 target butt with a 2-foot-square paper target for every four students
- 4 bale pins for each target

### Instructions to Class

- "Using good form, try to shoot your 6 arrows into the paper."
- "Keep your visual focus on the paper until your arrow lands."
- "Record the number of arrows striking paper in your first end."
- "Shoot 4 additional ends, trying to improve on your first-end score."

### Student Option

- None

### Student Success Goal

- 4 ends maintaining or increasing the number of arrows hitting paper in the standard end

### To Reduce Difficulty

- Drill is already in its simplest form.

### To Increase Difficulty

- Have your student draw a tic-tac-toe pattern on the paper. Students should then write "10" in the middle square, "4" in the corner squares, and "6" in the others. The archer totals the number of points earned on each end, trying to improve the score each time. [Corresponds to *Archery*, Step 4, Drill 4].

# 3. *Target Drill*

[Corresponds to *Archery*, Step 4, Drill 5]

## Group Management and Safety Tips

- Review scoring on a 5-color, 10-ring target.
- Place students in a straight line, three or four per target butt.
- Teacher stands behind students.
- Students shoot 5 ends of 6 arrows each from the 10-yard shooting line.
- Selectively watch shooters.

## Equipment

- Standard tackle for each student
- A 5-color, 10-ring, 80-cm target for each target butt
- 1 target butt and 4 bale pins for every four students in class
- Scoresheets

## Instructions to Class

- ''Using good form, try to shoot your 6 arrows as close to the bull's-eye as possible.''
- ''Keep your visual focus on the bull's-eye until your arrow lands.''
- ''Record your score on the first end.''
- ''Shoot 4 additional ends, trying to improve your first-end score.''

## Student Option

- ''Choose a partner. Shoot 6 ends, keeping the score of each end. When finished, flip a coin. If it is heads, add up each shooter's score on only the odd ends; if tails, add the even ends. Compare scores.'' [Corresponds to *Archery*, Step 4, Drill 6]

## Student Success Goal

- 4 ends with a higher score than the first end

## To Reduce Difficulty

- Students should shoot at a 122-cm target face.

## To Increase Difficulty

- Students should shoot from the 15-yard shooting line.

# 4. *Balloon Pop Drill*
[Corresponds to *Archery*, Step 4, Drill 7]

## Group Management and Safety Tips

- Have students blow up 6 balloons for every target butt and mount them with bale pins in the middle regions of the target butts.
- Place students in a straight line. Assign an equal number of students to each target. If any target is relatively short of archers, the number of its balloons can be reduced proportionately.
- Teacher stands behind students.
- Have students shoot 6-arrow ends from 10 yards.
- Selectively watch students.

## Equipment

- Archery tackle for every student
- 12 balloons for every four archers
- 1 target butt and 6 bale pins for each group of archers

## Instructions to Class

- ''Try to pop a balloon with each of your 6 shots.''
- ''See which group can pop all its balloons in the fewest number of ends.''

## Student Option

- None

## Student Success Goal

- Pop at least one of the balloons on the target butt.

## To Reduce Difficulty

- Use large balloons.

## To Increase Difficulty

- Use small balloons or don't inflate regular ones completely.
- Have your student shoot from the 15-yard shooting line.

# *Step 5*  Improving Shooting Accuracy

Shooting form is an important contribution to accuracy. The archer can add a variety of accessories, including a bowsight, to the basic archery tackle and can practice extensively to improve. Yet, a basic flaw in form will keep your student from reaching his or her full potential. Encourage your students to refine the basic shooting form before giving attention to accessories.

The rating chart below focuses upon several criteria for perfected form. Having worked with your students on the basics of shooting, turn now to perfecting these aspects of shooting, because they have a great impact on shooting accuracy.

## *Perfected Form Rating*

| CRITERION | BEGINNING LEVEL | INTERMEDIATE LEVEL | ADVANCED LEVEL |
|---|---|---|---|
| Draw | • Holds bow tightly with bow hand | • Starts with relaxed bow hand but grabs bow on release | • Holds bow with thumb and forefinger, keeping fingers and hand relaxed throughout shot |
| | • Lets upper body turn toward target | • Keeps shoulders square to target, but bow shoulder elevates in draw or aim phase | • Maintains T-alignment throughout shot |
| | • Uses arm muscles to draw | • Leans away from target | • Initiates draw with back muscles to move elbow back at shoulder level |
| | • Draw elbow may be too low | • Turns draw hand palm-down, torquing string | • Maintains relaxed, vertical draw hand |
| | • Has tension in draw hand | | |

## Perfected Form Rating

| CRITERION | BEGINNING LEVEL | INTERMEDIATE LEVEL | ADVANCED LEVEL |
|---|---|---|---|
| **Anchor and Aim** | • Fails to aim in predraw<br>• Anchor position is inconsistent from shot to shot<br>• Doesn't align arrow and bowstring<br>• Cants the bow<br><br>• Releases immediately after anchoring | • Aims in predraw<br><br>• Anchor position is consistent<br><br>• Occasionally forgets to align arrow and bowstring<br>• Holds the bow vertically<br><br>• Releases too quickly | • Aims in predraw<br><br>• Anchors consistently<br><br>• Consistently aligns the arrow and bowstring<br>• Takes time to steady and aim before release<br>• Increases back tension before release |
| **Release and Follow-Through** | • Has a jerky release<br><br>• Moves bow arm or head extensively on release | • Releases poorly on some shots<br>• Moves bow arm slightly on release | • Has a clean and smooth release<br>• Maintains bow arm and head position on release |

## Error Detection and Correction for Improving Shooting Accuracy

With practice and your feedback, the beginning archer is able to execute shots with good basic technique. Your student aligns his or her body in the proper orientation, can keep arrows on the arrow rest throughout the draw, shoots without the string striking the bow arm, and follows through.

There can still be flaws in technique, though, that are more subtle but undoubtedly affect accuracy. Continue to look for and correct the basic errors identified in previous steps, but look for the following errors in the archer who has established good basic form. Correcting these subtle errors will help the archer refine and perfect his or her form.

**ERROR**

**CORRECTION**

1. Archer holds the bow tightly or grabs the bow on release.

1. Have the archer hold the bow with the thumb and forefinger, keeping the other fingers relaxed. Student should try wiggling fingers after reaching full draw.

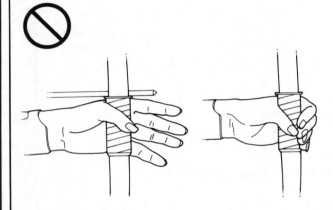

2. The archer has good alignment when anchoring, but gradually leans away from target or elevates front shoulder during the hold.

2. Encourage the archer to stay relaxed. After the shot is set up, the archer should steady, then release without waiting too long.

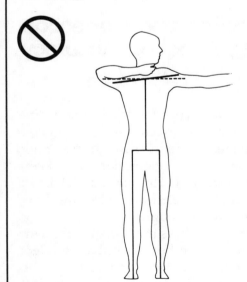

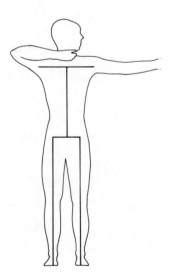

**ERROR**

**CORRECTION**

3. The release is jerky or the draw hand follow-through is not straight back.

3. This error can be caused by allowing tension in the draw hand during the draw and hold, which then can build up until release; emphasize forming a hook, but relaxing the rest of the draw hand throughout the shot, with release being a relaxation of the hook. A follow-through other than one straight back can also indicate a lack of back tension; emphasize drawing by use of the back muscles.

4. Archer varies anchor from shot to shot.

4. Emphasize the feel of the bowstring on the middle of the nose and chin, and of the chin on the hand. Remind the archer to close the mouth.

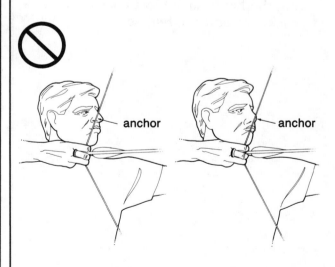

**ERROR**                                    **CORRECTION**

5. The bow is canted.

5. Remind the archer to look for the bow limbs in peripheral vision and straighten them.

6. Archer releases too quickly, before anchoring and steadying.

6. It may help to have the archer count silently to 3 before releasing, increasing the back tension on each count.

7. The arrow moves forward after the archer anchors.

7. The archer is losing back tension during the hold; have the archer increase back tension until release.

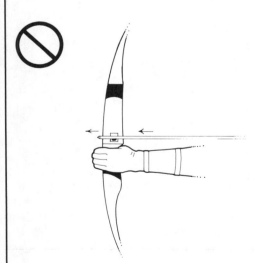

**ERROR**

**CORRECTION**

8. Archer turns the draw hand slightly palm-down during the hold or in follow-through.

8. This places a torque on the string. Have the archer hook onto the string with the hand vertical and maintain this position. An archer with this habit may have to feel like he or she is turning the hand under in order to achieve a vertical position.

# Selected Drills
# for Improving Shooting Accuracy

## *1. Relaxed Bow Hand Check*
[Corresponds to *Archery*, Step 5, Drills 2 and 3]

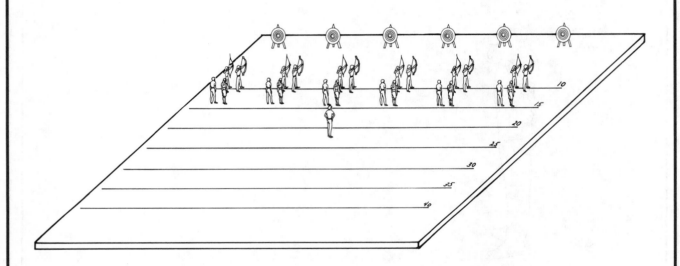

## Group Management and Safety Tips

- Distribute two dot stickers to each archer.
- Students should pair up.
- Class should shoot from the 10-yard shooting line.
- Remind observing partner to stay behind the archer.

## Equipment

- 2 dot stickers per student
- Standard archery tackle for every student
- 1 target butt, an 80-cm target face, and 4 bale pins for every four students

## Instructions to Class

- "Place one sticker on your bow handle, above the grip, then take your shooting position and place the other sticker on your hand, aligned with the bow sticker."
- "One partner shoots first, and the other observes."
- "Shoot 6-arrow ends, lining up the stickers on every shot."
- "Observing partners should say 'hold' on selected shots and brush the archer's bow-hand fingers to see whether they are relaxed."

### Student Option

- ''Purchase an accessory for the bow that is a self-adhering piece of leather with a raised ridge running lengthwise. Place the piece on the bow handle such that the ridge is centered in the palm when the bow is held properly. Feel for this ridge to be in a consistent position on each shot.''

### Student Keys to Success

- Set bow hand
- Form loose ring with bow thumb and index finger
- Relax bow hand
- Maintain relaxed bow hand

### Student Success Goals

- Every shot with a perfectly aligned bow hand
- Have a relaxed bow hand on two thirds of the shots checked

### To Reduce Difficulty

- Check for relaxed bow hand once after archer shoots 4 ends using the stickers to duplicate the bow-hand position.

### To Increase Difficulty

- Make your students shoot for an extended time and try to maintain a relaxed bow hand.

## 2. Follow-Through Drill
[Corresponds to *Archery*, Step 5, Drill 4]

### Group Management and Safety Tips

- Have students pair up in groups of 4, alternately shooting and observing.
- Teacher stands behind students.
- Class shoots 6-arrow ends from the 10-yard line.
- Each archer should shoot at least 2 ends.
- Observing partner should stand behind archer.

### Equipment

- Standard tackle for every student
- 1 target butt, an 80-cm target face, and 4 bale pins for every four students

### Instructions to Class

- ''Shooters, maintain a good follow-through position until your partner tells you to relax.''
- ''Observers, wait 3–5 seconds before saying 'relax.' ''

### Student Option

- None

### Student Keys to Success

- Relax draw hand to release string
- Draw elbow pulls back on release
- Keep bow arm up and toward target
- Maintain head position
- Draw hand finishes over rear shoulder

### Student Success Goal

- 10 shots with perfect follow-through maintained until the relax cue out of 12 total shots

### To Reduce Difficulty

- The student should make sure that back muscles are used to draw and that good T-alignment is used. When other muscles are used and the body is out of alignment, it is difficult to have a good follow-through.

### To Increase Difficulty

- When your student can easily perform this drill, move him or her on to the following drills.

# 3. Grouping Drill
[Corresponds to *Archery*, Step 5, Drill 5]

## Group Management and Safety Tips

- Assign four archers to each target. Distribute a tape measure to each group.
- Each student will shoot 5 ends of 6 arrows each from the 10-yard line.
- Any large target face can be used.
- Selectively assist students.

## Equipment

- Standard archery tackle for every student
- 1 target butt, 1 target face, 4 bale pins, and 1 tape measure for every four students

## Instructions to Class

- "Score your shots by measuring around your entire group of 6 arrows with the tape measure."
- "The lower your measurement, the better."
- "Pull the arrows out after you measure."
- "Your first score is a reference end to which you will compare successive ends."

## Student Option

- "Use a piece of string 2 feet in length to surround the arrow group. Count only those arrows that can be encircled by the string."

## Student Keys to Success

- Relax the bow hand
- Relax the draw hand to release
- Keep the bow arm up, toward the target
- Maintain head position

## Student Success Goal

- 4 ends with a better score (lower measurement) than the reference end

## To Reduce Difficulty

- This is already the simplest form of the drill.

## To Increase Difficulty

- Have your student shoot from the 15-yard line.

# 4. Symbol Target
[Corresponds to *Archery*, Step 5, Drill 6]

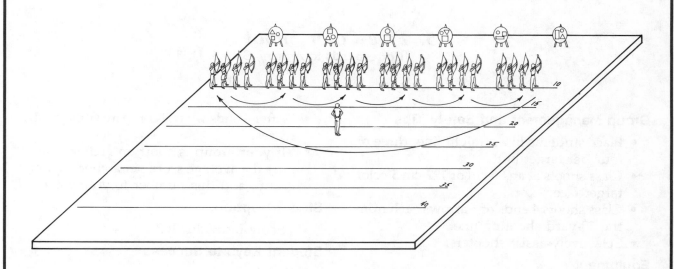

## Group Management and Safety Tips

- Place students in groups of three to four. Distribute a large piece of heavy paper and a felt marker to each group.
- All groups should hang their targets before the class is ready to shoot.
- Class will shoot 6-arrow ends from the 10-yard shooting line.
- After scoring each end, groups rotate one target butt to the right, with the group farthest right coming back to the first target butt on the left.

## Equipment

- Standard archery tackle
- Scoresheets for each group of three to four archers
- 1 target butt, 1 large sheet of heavy paper, 4 bale pins, and 1 felt marker for each group

## Instructions to Class

- "Draw various symbols on your paper, making them large enough to hit with your shots. When you are finished, hang your target butt."
- "Record the number of symbols on your target hit or touched by all the archers. Count symbols twice if two archers hit them or one archer hits a symbol with two arrows."

- "Shoot 1 end at every target butt."
- "Your group score will be compared with other groups when you're finished."
- "If your group is short an archer, compute the average number of symbols struck by your group; add this number to your total."

## Student Options

- "Keep individual scores."
- "Shoot at each target a second time."

## Student Keys to Success

- Toes aligned
- Stand erect
- Elbow back at shoulder level
- Follow through

## Student Success Goal

- Your group hits more symbols than any other group

## To Reduce Difficulty

- Let your student turn the paper over and draw the symbols bigger.

## To Increase Difficulty

- Have your student turn the paper over and draw the symbols smaller.
- Make your student shoot from the 15-yard line.

# 5. *Five-Color Shoot*

[Corresponds to *Archery*, Step 5, Drill 7]

### Group Management and Safety Tips

- Place students in a straight line, three or four per target butt.
- Class shoots at an 80-cm or 122-cm 5-color target face.
- Class shoots 4 ends of 6 arrows each from the 10-yard shooting line.
- Selectively assist shooters.

### Equipment

- Standard archery tackle
- 1 target butt, an 80-cm or 122-cm 5-color target, and 4 bale pins for every group of three or four students
- Cards or paper with the names of each of the five target colors (white, black, blue, red, gold) written on them, and a container for them
- Scoresheets for each group

### Instructions to Class

- ''Before you go forward to score, a paper will be pulled from a hat. There are 5 papers, each with the name of a color written on it. You should double the value of any arrows in the color pulled from the hat. Circle the doubled arrows on your scoresheet.''
- ''After 4 ends we will compare your group scores.''
- ''If your group is short an archer, compute the average score per archer in your group; add this number to your total.''

### Student Option

- ''Score individually.''

### Student Keys to Success

- Weight even
- Elbow back
- String on chin and nose
- Increase back tension
- Relax draw hand to release
- Follow through

### Student Success Goal

- Your group accumulating more points than other groups

### To Reduce Difficulty

- Drill is already in its simplest form.

### To Increase Difficulty

- Have your student shoot from the 15-yard line.

# *Step 6*   Adding Basic Accessories

When your students can handle their equipment comfortably and shoot with good form, several basic accessories can help them score better. Students enjoy archery more when they score well; providing these accessories can add to their enjoyment and motivate them to practice.

The accessories that can be introduced at this point in your students' learning are the bowsight, peep sight, kisser button, and bow sling. Many types of each are on the market. Although bowsights can be very expensive, many low-cost models are available and more than adequate for beginning students. The other accessories are relatively inexpensive. If cost would keep you from providing these items for your students, you should consider making bowsights, bow slings, and kisser buttons. Directions for making these accessories and directions for installing all four items follow.

## THE BOWSIGHT

A bowsight is an important addition to the archer's equipment. With a sight, the archer can consistently direct arrows to the target, and make systematic adjustments in aiming. Although some archers enjoy the challenge of shooting ''bare bow,'' without a sight, most find it more rewarding to shoot with the consistency of aim that a sight affords. The beginning archer typically enjoys the increased success that comes with the addition of a bowsight.

A good rule of thumb for purchasing bowsights, either individually or for a class, is to buy the best that you can afford to buy. High-quality sights are durable and can be adjusted consistently. However, inexpensive and homemade sights also do a good job, and it is undoubtedly better to make your own sights than not to provide students with bowsights.

## Installing a Purchased Bowsight

A manufactured bowsight is mounted on either the back of the bow, the side away from the archer, the face of the bow, or an extension bar via a sight bracket mounted on the side of the bow opposite the bow window. A bow with metal handle risers is usually pre-tapped for screws that hold the sight bracket for an extension sight permanently in place. Laminated wood and fiberglass bows and solid fiberglass bows must be tapped.

If you are using laminated or solid fiberglass bows, it is best to purchase sights that mount directly onto them. A sight extended out from a bow on an extension bar obviously is heavier and best attached to a metal handle riser. You do not have to purchase sights in right- or left-handed models; the sight apertures can be reversed to accommodate archers from either side.

A bowsight can be mounted on the face or the back of the bow. The advantage of a face mount is that the shorter distance between the archer's eye and the sight results in the sight aperture being placed higher on the sight bar to achieve a given angle of elevation. Therefore, sight settings for long distances can be obtained without interfering with the flight of the arrow upon release.

The main advantage of a back mount is that the longer distance between eye and sight provides the opportunity for finer aiming, and less adverse effect if release occurs when the sight is not perfectly aimed. In class situations, you are likely to have light-poundage bows and to shoot at shorter distances (40 yards or less) anyway, and you should take advantage of the finer aiming that back mounts provide. In making your decision on where to mount your sights, consider, too, that a bowsight is better protected during storage and transportation when mounted on the face of the bow;

if you make your own sights, which are more delicate than manufactured sights, you may want to mount them on the face. The following instructions are for a back mount but are easily converted for a front mount.

Position the bowsight on the back of the bow at the level of the sight window. Mark the bow location of the sight's lower screw with a pencil. Drill a small hole at this mark. It is best to use small hardware in order to avoid splitting the bow or structurally weakening it. Position the bowsight again and carefully attach the bottom end with a screw here.

Lay the bow on a table and place a level on the bowstring. Shim the bow by placing objects under it to level the string, if necessary. Now place the level on the sight and pivot the sight until it is also level. Mark the top drill hole. This assures that the sight is parallel to the bowstring and that the left-right sight setting will remain the same as the archer shoots different distances and moves the sight aperture up and down. Drill the top hole and attach the top end of the sight with a small screw (see Figure 6.1).

**Figure 6.1** An inexpensive sight, attached to the bow with two small screws.

Bowsights can be taped onto the bow with vinyl tape if you are reluctant to drill holes in your bows. Obviously, though, taped sights require more maintenance than those permanently attached.

## Making Your Own Bowsights

You can make bowsights quite easily and inexpensively. Make one for each bow and keep extra materials on hand for replacement and repair.

### Materials Needed for Each Bowsight

- 5 inches of weather-stripping foam, preferably self-adhering
- 5 inches of vinyl tape in a light color
- 5 inches of double-sided tape, if foam is not self-adhering
- Black, permanent-ink felt marker
- Straight pin with a long stem and ball head
- A metric ruler

### Bowsight Procedure

1. Cut a 5-inch piece of weather-stripping foam from the roll and peel off the protective paper. A piece of felt can be substituted for foam weather stripping, but the foam stays in place better than felt, especially with prolonged use.
2. Stick the foam strip onto the back of the bow at the level of the sight window and parallel to the bowstring. If your weather stripping is not self-adhering, attach it with double-sided tape.
3. Cover the foam strip with a 5-inch piece of vinyl tape.
4. Place the metric ruler next to the tape and place a short line every half-centimeter with your felt marker. Number these lines from 1 to approximately 25. These will serve as reference marks when your students establish sight settings for various shooting distances.

5. Insert the straight pin into the foam from the sight window side to serve as an aiming aperture (see Figure 6.2). Its location up and down the foam strip provides an elevation setting, and the distance it is pushed into the foam provides a lateral setting. The pin should be angled down and pushed all the way into the foam for transportation and storage.

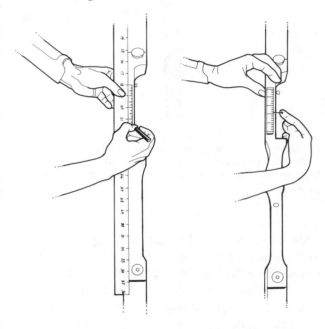

**Figure 6.2**  A sight can be made by attaching a strip of insulation foam to the bow, covering it with a piece of vinyl tape, and marking half-inch increments on the tape. A straight pin with a ball head serves as the aiming aperture.

## THE PEEP SIGHT

The peep sight adds to the accuracy of aiming. This small disc is placed between the strands of the bowstring and has a small hole through which the archer looks to align the sight aperture. Not only does it act as a rear sight, but it allows the archer to look through the bowstring rather than to the side of it. The archer can be more precise in aligning the bull's-eye and sight aperture in the center of the peep sight than in aligning the blurry image of the string near their eye to the side of the aperture.

On the other hand, some tournament rules exclude the peep sight. Also, patience and experimentation are needed to set the peep sight properly. It is typically used with compound bows. You might want to wait until your archers master use of the bowsight and decide which equipment style interests them the most before introducing the peep sight. Also, the location of the peep sight is likely to change if an archer later changes the anchor position.

Peep sights are a relatively inexpensive accessory to purchase; very few archers make their own peep sights. The peep sight must be strong because it is placed between the strands of the bowstring and, when it is tied into position, the string exerts pressure on it. Hard plastic and metal are the materials most commonly used in the manufacture of peep sights. The sides of the peep sight must also be very smooth so that the bowstring is not cut or excessively worn.

Peep sights are available with viewing holes of various diameters. The size used is largely a matter of personal preference for the archer, but one using the fingers to hold and release the bowstring usually chooses a larger diameter. The bowstring usually twists to some extent when the fingers are placed on the string to draw it back to the anchor position. There is naturally a small variation in the extent to which it twists from shot to shot; the larger hole makes it easier to accommodate this variation.

The archer using a mechanical release often chooses a small diameter hole because the string does not twist when drawn with a release, and the smaller hole allows for even finer aiming. Many hunters and some target archers use a type of peep sight that is attached to rubber tubing mounted on the upper bow limb; this tubing pulls the peep sight around to the proper orientation on every shot so that the shot need never be started over because the peep sight is not aligned.

### Positioning the Peep Sight

In order to help a student position a peep sight correctly, you should stand next to him or her on the shooting line. Spread the strands of the bowstring apart, with about half the strands on each side, and insert the peep sight; place it at a point that will be about eye level. The archer should draw and anchor as normal. After anchoring, move the peep sight up or down until your student reports that he or she can center the bull's-eye and sight aperture in the peep sight. You might also have to twist the string to orient the peep sight properly. The archer should then carefully let the bow down. You might have to repeat this several times to achieve the ideal position and to recheck it.

Once the correct position is obtained, mark the bowstring at this location. If a student is using personal equipment or you can dedicate use of a bow to a single student, the peep sight can be tied into location permanently. If you or the archer would like to hold the peep sight in place but also be able to move it at a later time, the following method of tying is ideal; these ties can be moved if desired, but they hold the peep sight in place relatively well in the meantime.

### Tying the Peep Sight

Obtain two pieces of nylon serving thread, the kind used to serve a bowstring, about 18 inches in length. One will be tied above the peep sight and one below. Starting below the peep sight, place the thread around the bowstring and tie an overhand knot (the first action in tying a shoelace, before tying the bows) on your side of the string. Now take each end of the thread around opposite sides of the bowstring and tie another overhand knot on the side away from you. Continue tying overhand knots on opposite sides of the string, working down the string, until the entire knot is about a half-inch in length. Cut off the excess thread and carefully melt the free ends back to the last knot with a match. Repeat this on the other side of the peep sight (above it), working up the string (see Figure 6.3).

Once the peep sight is at the correct elevation, you still might have to adjust its orientation to compensate for any twist the archer puts onto the string while hooking onto it and drawing. An archer using the fingers to hold

**Figure 6.3** The peep sight is inserted between strands of the string. Two pieces of bowstring serving are knotted above and below it to hold the disc in place.

the bowstring usually has the peep sight offset slightly to the right (if right-handed, because the string is twisted slightly left when he or she hooks and draws). Determining this position is usually a trial-and-error procedure in which you must remove one end of the string and twist it before replacing it.

You can now see why the peep sight is typically used with a compound bow: These adjustments are more easily made with the compound bow because a spare string can be placed on the cables while the original string is turned. Also, once the position is set, the bowstring is left as is because the compound bow is not unstrung between shooting sessions.

### THE KISSER BUTTON

The kisser button greatly helps archers achieve a consistent anchor on every shot. If equipment is shared among archers, however, several problems arise. First, the location of the kisser button is specific to each archer, and it is unlikely that any two archers sharing equipment need it in the same place. Second, the kisser button should be wiped down with isopropyl alcohol for each new archer if equipment is shared. These are not insurmountable problems; it might well be worth overcoming them to provide this valuable aid to students.

Kisser buttons are a relatively inexpensive accessory. They come in sizes by diameter, and you should purchase the small size of about 1 cm in diameter if your students participate in events governed by Federation Internationale de Tir a L'Arc (FITA) regulations. One kisser button for each bow plus a half-dozen extras should be purchased.

Two types of kisser buttons are available. One has a slit and is slipped easily onto the string. It is then clamped down with a small C ring and a pair of nocking pliers.

The other type of kisser button does not have a slit, and it must be threaded onto the string. This type is more difficult to install. However, particularly if equipment is shared among archers, it will probably be tight enough to stay in place when archers position it for themselves. The best way to install a kisser button is to position a hairpin on the bowstring, over the dacron strands; slip the kisser button over the hairpin, then over the bowstring until it passes over the bowstring loop.

## Making Your Own Kisser Buttons

If you are unable to purchase kisser buttons, you can make them very easily. These home-made kisser buttons are tight enough on the string to allow archers to share equipment by sliding the kisser button up or down just before they shoot.

### Materials Needed

- Truck innertube or equivalent piece of rubber
- Hole punch (approximately 1/2 inch)
- Ice pick
- Hammer

### Kisser Button Procedure

1. Place the piece of rubber over a section of scrap wood. Punch out the number of kisser buttons needed with the hole punch and hammer (see Figure 6.4).

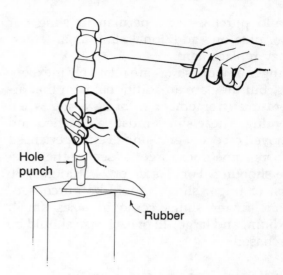

**Figure 6.4** Handmade kisser buttons can be made by punching a small disc from a piece of rubber.

2. Punch a small hole in the center of each kisser button with an ice pick.
3. Use the hairpin method described above to position the kisser buttons on the bowstrings.
4. If the kisser button will be anchored in one location on the string, give students two long pieces of dental floss or nylon wrapping thread. They can wrap a piece around the bowstring just above and another just below the kisser button, then knot them to hold the kisser button in place.

## THE BOW SLING

You have a choice of purchasing bow slings that are permanently attached to your bows, or slings that archers attach to their wrists or fingers after taking their grips. Generally, one attached to a bow itself is more expensive, but will not be lost and can be adjusted to fit archers of any size. One type of permanent sling has adhesive backing and attaches directly to the bow handle. Another type attaches at the stabilizer insert, obviously requiring that the bow be tapped for a stabilizer. Both kinds have adjustable straps through which archers slide their bow hands as they take their grips. The straps can be adjusted in length. You should purchase one permanent sling per bow, plus one additional sling as an emergency replacement.

Finger or wrist slings are relatively inexpensive, but they are an additional item that archers must remember to bring along when shooting. These slings must be attached and removed on every end, and even experienced archers sometimes forget to secure them before shooting. For classes of 24 students, 30 wrist or finger slings should be purchased. Plastic finger slings come in sizes small, medium, and large; 12 of each size should be purchased.

## Making Your Own Wrist Slings

If funds are not available for purchasing bow or wrist slings, wrist slings can be made relatively easily and inexpensively. They are made in three sizes, and it is best to make 12 of each size for classes of 24, in which archers are bound to vary in size.

### Materials Needed

- 66 feet of nylon cord
- 36 lanyard hooks
- A candle

### Wrist Sling Procedure

1. Cut the nylon cord as follows:

   12 pieces 20 inches in length
   12 pieces 22 inches in length
   12 pieces 24 inches in length

2. Use the candle to melt the ends of each piece of cord to keep it from fraying.
3. Tie a slip knot with one end of each piece of cord to form a loop big enough to fit over the hand (see Figure 6.5).
4. Slip the lanyard hook over the other end of the cord. Bend the small end of the hook, leaving a 1/4-inch opening at the large end.
5. Slip your hand through the large loop. Using a class bow, assume a bow-hand grip and tighten the slip knot. Bring the hook end of the cord between your fingers and around the bow, hooking the lanyard hook onto the cord around the wrist.

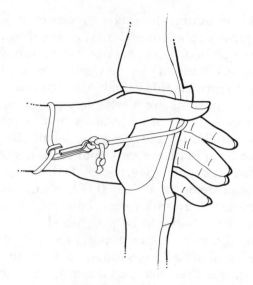

**Figure 6.5** A handmade wrist sling is wrapped around the hand and bow handle, then attached to the wrist loop on the inside of the wrist.

6. Adjust the position of the lanyard hook on the cord to make the sling secure but not too tight. Tie a knot at the lanyard hook, holding it in place.
7. Tie a small knot in the end of the cord to keep the end from sliding through the lanyard hook knot.

The addition of some or all of these accessories should contribute to the success of your students. You can now begin to challenge them further by shooting from various distances and to smaller targets. You can also begin to use scores to assess student performance.

# Step 7 Using a Bowsight

The use of a bowsight is a great boost to shooting accuracy. Once an archer can execute the basic shot with good technique, learning to aim a bowsight allows near-maximal shooting accuracy with the equipment available. There are several aspects of sighting that must be executed properly to achieve this level of performance. Archers will be at various levels in learning to use a bowsight, to aim, and to steady their shots. You can use the following chart to assess novice archers who are learning these skills.

## STUDENT KEYS TO SUCCESS

- Draw and anchor
- Close left eye if necessary (right-handed archer)
- Align right eye with sight and bull's-eye
- Level bow
- Adjust head to see string bisecting bow and just to right of aperture (or center target in peep sight)
- Focus on bull's-eye
- Steady sight aperture in middle of bull's-eye

## Using a Bowsight Rating

| CRITERION | BEGINNING LEVEL | INTERMEDIATE LEVEL | ADVANCED LEVEL |
|---|---|---|---|
| **Sighting (at full draw)** | • Cants bow<br><br>• Sometimes aims with wrong eye<br><br>• Doesn't align bowstring with middle of bow<br>• Fails to align bowstring with aiming aperture<br><br>• Focuses on aiming aperture<br>• Shoots before sight aperture is aligned with bull's-eye<br>or<br>• Fails to use sight at all | • Levels bow<br><br>• Almost always aims with draw-side eye<br>• Aligns bowstring with middle of bow<br>• Puts bowstring on wrong side of aiming aperture<br><br>• Focuses on bull's-eye<br>• Shoots before sight aperture is steadied in bull's-eye | • Levels bow<br><br>• Always aims with draw-side eye<br>• Aligns bowstring with middle of bow<br>• Aligns bowstring to right of aiming aperture (if right-handed)<br>• Focuses on bull's eye<br>• Allows aiming aperture to steady in bull's-eye before release |
| **Sight Adjustment (after shot)** | • Moves aperture opposite the direction of error | • Sometimes confuses direction of adjustment, especially left-right when turning bow around to adjust sight | • Moves aperture in the direction of error |

# Error Detection and Correction for Using a Bowsight

There are several typical errors associated with sighting and aiming that novice archers make. Look for these errors in particular while your students are learning to use bowsights. The suggested corrections assume that the student in question has good form, that is, that the error is related only to the sighting and aiming process and is not a technique flaw.

**ERROR**

**CORRECTION**

| ERROR | CORRECTION |
| --- | --- |
| 1. The directional error of arrows is accentuated after a sight adjustment. | 1. Check to see that the adjustment was made in the correct direction (direction of error). Suggest that the archer keep the bow in the same orientation as when shooting so that left and right are not confused by turning the bow around to face the sight scale. Show the archer how moving the sight one direction points the bow the opposite direction. |
| 2. The archer releases before steadying and aiming the shot. | 2. This is a form of target panic. Have the archer practice the Holding Drill (in the participant's book) at the beginning of each practice session. If the problem persists, the archer will benefit from using a clicker accessory. |
| 3. Some arrows land near the bull's-eye, and some extremely right or left. | 3. The student may be aligning the wrong eye with the sight on some shots. Have the student close the nonaiming eye or, if this is uncomfortable, use an eye patch. |
| 4. The archer inhales before aiming and release, and the arrow on such a shot lands high. | 4. The archer should inhale before the draw then exhale some, but not all, air before aiming and releasing. |
| 5. Arrows spread across the target horizontally. | 5. The archer may not be aligning the bowstring consistently. The archer should practice the Aiming Mimic Drill and include a mental reminder to align the string in every shot sequence. |

# Selected Sighting and Aiming Drills

## 1. *Aiming Mimic*
[Corresponds to *Archery*, Step 7, Drill 1]

### Group Management and Safety Tips

- Review sight and string alignment for shooting with a sight.
- Students should take position in a single line, in front of targets.
- Selectively stand uprange from archers to check their alignment.

### Equipment

- Bows (equipped with sights) and finger tabs for every student
- 1 target butt with mounted target face for every four students

### Instructions to Class

- "Without an arrow, practice drawing; anchoring; aligning the sight aperture, bull's-eye, and bowstring; aiming; and steadying."
- "Ease the string back, rest, and repeat."

### Student Option

- None

### Student Keys to Success

- Draw and anchor
- Close left eye (if right-handed)
- Align right eye with sight and bull's-eye
- Level bow
- See string bisect bow and to right of sight aperture (or center peep sight)
- Focus on bull's-eye
- Steady sight
- Count to 3

### Student Success Goal

- 10 repetitions with steady aiming and perfect alignment

### To Reduce Difficulty

- Drill is already in its simplest form.

### To Increase Difficulty

- Have your student actually shoot arrows (from 10 yards; target area should be clear).

## 2. *Sighting In*
[Corresponds to *Archery*, Step 7, Drill 3]

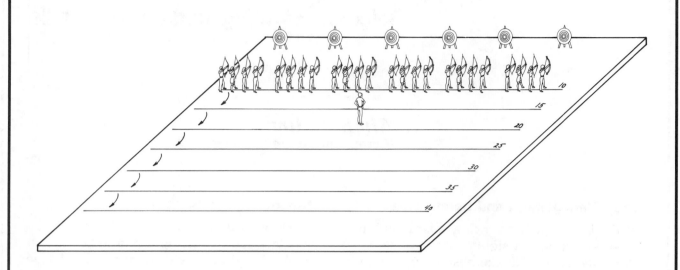

### Group Management and Safety Tips

- Have students check the sights on their bows to be sure they are in working order.
- Review rules for adjusting sights in the direction of arrow error.
- Have students shoot from the 10-yard line to obtain and record their sight settings for this distance. Two or more ends may be necessary to obtain the sight setting. Repeat this process for each distance to 40 yards in 5-yard increments.
- Everyone in the class should shoot from the same distance unless an empty target can be left between the targets of students shooting distances 5 yards apart.

### Equipment

- Standard archery tackle, including bowsights, for every student
- Paper and pencil for recording sight settings
- 1 target butt, an 80-cm target face, and 4 bale pins for every four students

### Instructions to Class

- "Place the sight aperture on your bow high on the sight bar about 5 inches above the arrow rest height."
- "Shoot 3 arrows from 10 yards."
- "Adjust your sight according to the error of your arrow group."
- "Continue to adjust your sight setting during the first two ends, basing your sight adjustments on shots you execute well."
- "Record the vertical setting for your shooting at 10 yards."
- "Move back 5 yards, move your sight down a small amount, and repeat this process."

### Student Option

- "Graph your sight settings relative to the corresponding distances to see whether all the settings fall along a straight or curved line."

### Student Success Goal

- Obtain an accurate sight setting for each distance

### To Reduce Difficulty

- Student should get sight settings for 10, 20, 30, and 40 yards, then only estimate the settings for 15, 25, and 35 yards.

### To Increase Difficulty

- Make your student also obtain sight settings for 45 and 50 yards.

## 3. Square Target Drill
[Corresponds to *Archery*, Step 7, Drill 5]

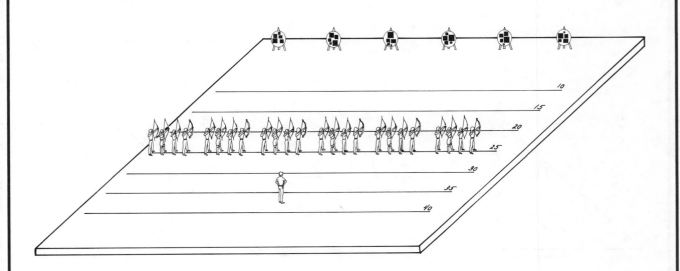

### Group Management and Safety Tips

- Students need 25-yard sight settings for this drill.
- Assign three or four archers per target.
- Students assigned to a specified target should draw squares, with the help of the patterns you provide, onto a large sheet of paper.
- Have students shoot from the 25-yard line.

### Equipment

- Standard archery tackle
- 1 target butt, 1 large sheet of heavy paper, 4 bale pins, and 1 felt marker for every four archers
- Cardboard patterns in the following sizes: 9 × 9 in., 8 × 8 in., 7 × 7 in., 6 × 6 in., and 5 × 5 in.

### Instructions to Class

- ''Make your target by using the square patterns and writing '10' under the smallest square, '9' under the second smallest, and so on.''

- ''Hang your target.''
- ''Shoot 6-arrow ends, keeping score according to the value of the squares in which your arrows land. Keep a running score and see who in your foursome can reach 100 points first.''

### Student Option

- ''Shoot from another distance.''

### Student Success Goal

- 100 points with fewer arrows than the other archers assigned to the same target

### To Reduce Difficulty

- Let your student shoot from a shorter distance.
- Have student make larger squares.

### To Increase Difficulty

- Make your student shoot from a longer distance.
- Have student make the squares smaller.

# 4. Dart Board Game

[Corresponds to *Archery*, Step 7, Drill 6]

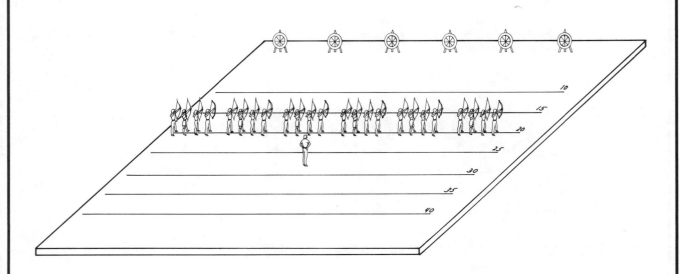

### Group Management and Safety Tips

- Students should have a 20-yard sight setting.
- Place students in a single line, three or four per target.
- Students assigned to a target should draw a large circle (about 60 cm in diameter) on a large sheet of heavy paper, divide the circle into 8 ''pie slices,'' and randomly number the slices from 1 to 8.
- All students should shoot 4 six-arrow ends from the 20-yard line.

### Equipment

- Standard archery tackle
- 1 target butt, 1 large sheet of heavy paper, 4 bale pins, and 1 felt marker for every four archers

### Instructions to Class

- ''Make your dart board target and hang it on your target butt.''
- ''Record your score on each end.''
- ''Try to improve your score on each successive end.''

### Student Option

- ''Shoot from various distances.''

### Student Success Goal

- Increase your score on successive ends

### To Reduce Difficulty

- Let your student make the circle larger.
- Have student shoot from a shorter distance.

### To Increase Difficulty

- Have student make circle smaller.
- Make your student shoot from a longer distance.

## 5. *Quick Sight Move*
[Corresponds to *Archery*, Step 7, Drill 7]

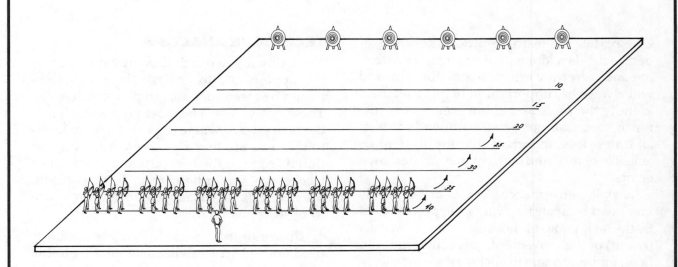

### Group Management and Safety Tips

- Students need sight settings for all distances from 20–40 yards in 5-yard increments.
- Assign three or four students to each target.
- Allow students a practice end at 40 yards.
- Have students shoot 1 six-arrow end at each distance from 40–20 yards in 5-yard increments, then return to 40 yards and repeat.
- Students should score their arrows from 10 points to 1 point on the 10-ring target face.
- All students shoot from the same distance at the same time.
- Selectively assist students.

### Equipment

- Standard archery tackle
- 1 target butt, an 80-cm target face, and 4 bale pins for every four archers

### Instructions to Class

- ''Take a 6-arrow practice end at 40 yards.''
- ''Shoot one end at each distance from 40–20 yards in 5-yard increments, adjusting your sight settings as necessary.''
- ''Use 10-ring scoring to keep score on each end. Total your score.''
- ''Move back to 40 yards and repeat, trying to improve your score.''

### Student Option

- ''Take written note of ends in which the arrow group is high or low (and not attributable to a form error) and adjust the sight setting as necessary on the second round.''

### Student Success Goal

- Shoot a better score in the second round than the first

### To Reduce Difficulty

- Have student use a 122-cm target.

### To Increase Difficulty

- Make archer use a 60-cm target at 25 and 20 yards.

## *Step 8*  Detecting and Correcting Errors

One part of the learning process for the student is the development of a system for detecting and correcting errors. Instructors are, and will always be, important in helping learners identify their mistakes. However, an instructor or coach cannot be at a student's side at all times. It is important that the student be able to detect and correct his or her own errors.

In skill performance, errors are typically identified by analyzing either the process (that is, the technique) of movement or the product (result) of the movement. It is sometimes difficult for performers to analyze their own techniques because they do not see themselves perform. Photographs and videotapes can be used, however. The performance product is somewhat easier to examine, but performers must know how results are related to technique. For example, a javelin thrower might see that the trajectory of a given throw was too flat. The thrower must then know how to produce a throw with a larger takeoff angle.

In archery, a process analysis usually takes the form of rating each phase of the technique in executing a shot—stance, draw and anchor, and release and follow-through. A product analysis could take the form of examining the score, but score alone does not tell the archer how to change his or her technique. An alternative is to examine the pattern the arrows form on the target face when shot in a group of 3-6.

*Archery: Steps to Success* provides students with two sections of information for detecting and correcting errors. One is a technique analysis, and the other an arrow analysis. Now you will learn some hints for working with students on these two types of analyses. By doing so, you will help students develop their own systems for detecting and correcting errors.

### TECHNIQUE ANALYSIS

The following two activities provide students the opportunity to analyze their own techniques by means of photographs or videotape. These analyses will be most productive if students first learn where to position themselves to take one another's pictures. You will also find these to be the best positions from which to observe and critique their form yourself. There are six beneficial positions from which to observe, as follows:

*1. Downrange:* The downrange position is used only when an archer is mimicking a shot without an arrow. The observer is positioned between the archer and the target, facing the archer from about 10 feet. This is an excellent place from which to check upper-body alignment. If the observer can see the archer's rear shoulder, the archer is not in line. It is easy to see, too, whether the archer is hunching the shoulders; consequently, the bow itself would not be in line with the archer's body (see Figure 8.1).

**Figure 8.1**  The downrange observation position gives this view of the archer.

**2. Front:** In the front position, the observer faces the archer from approximately 15 feet up the shooting line. For photographs and videotapes, the distance can be adjusted for the particular camera so that the archer can be seen from head to foot and arm to arm. Then the photographer can move in for close-ups of the anchor position and bow hand. This is a good position for judging erect posture, height of the draw elbow, and head position (see Figure 8.2).

**Figure 8.2** The front observation position gives this view of the archer.

**3. Rear:** The rear position is opposite the front position, approximately 15 feet down the shooting line. Photographs or videotapes should include a full view and perhaps a close-up of the bow hand. Many of the same features can be seen here as in the front position, but more attention can be given to body position and follow-through without the distraction of the anchor and release (see Figure 8.3).

**Figure 8.3** The rear observation position gives this view of the archer.

**4. Uprange:** An important observation position is uprange, about 10 feet directly behind the archer (relative to the target). From here an observer can sight downrange to the target, checking upper-body and stance alignment. This is also a good position from which to check for bow cant, body posture, head position, and head movement in the follow-through (see Figure 8.4).

**Figure 8.4** The uprange observation position gives this view of the archer.

**5. Oblique:** It is beneficial to observe from uprange but slightly to the front side and at close range. This position provides a close view of the bow arm and hand, the anchor, and the draw hand. In fact, the observer can see the inside of the draw hand by crouching slightly. Photographers can get several worthwhile close-ups here (see Figure 8.5).

**Figure 8.5** The oblique observation position gives this view of the archer.

**6. Above:** One of the best observation positions is uprange but 2–4 feet higher than the archer. This is not the easiest position to arrange, but often a ladder, officiating stand, or stable chair is available. This above position provides a good view of alignment during the draw and anchor as well as side movements during the release and follow-through (see Figure 8.6).

**Figure 8.6** The above observation position gives this view of the archer.

## Analyzing Photographs and Videotapes

Videotaping is the preferred medium for photographing shooting form. The release can be captured with the video camera, whereas still photographs often miss this action. It is particularly beneficial to view the videotape on a player with slow motion or frame-by-frame advance because the release and any accompanying movement can be better seen. If a video camera is unavailable, though, still photographs can provide much information about alignment and follow-through position.

Whether a video or picture camera is used, a zoom lens is preferred. Some full-length shots of the archer are needed, but close-ups, especially of the draw and bow hands, are useful. It is ideal to photograph close-ups without being so close as to disturb the archer.

When still photographs are available, archers should take advantage of this medium by drawing alignment lines directly on the photos. For example, the lines drawn on a photo taken from the front position should follow the shoulder level, hips, trunk, and legs. T-alignment of the shoulders with the trunk and erect posture can be checked more easily with this aid (see Figure 8.7).

**Figure 8.7** Students can superimpose straight lines on a photograph of themselves in order to check for T-alignment.

It is usually difficult to see small movements on videotape. For example, the bow arm might drop only 2 inches on release. This would be large enough to affect the arrow shot but small enough to be overlooked on videotape. A method of overcoming this problem is to videotape against a backdrop of vertical and level horizontal lines. A posture analysis chart can be used. Otherwise, make a backdrop by hanging a white sheet or pieces of large sign paper from a coatrack and drawing or taping black lines on this background (see Figure 8.8).

**Figure 8.8** When videotaping, it helps to place the archer in front of a grid. Alignment deviations and slight movements are easier to detect with the grid.

### The Technique Analysis Chart

The Technique Analysis Chart (shown with Drills 1 and 2, and also described in the ''Evaluation Ideas'' section later in this book) can be used with photographs and videotapes. The Technique Analysis Chart suggests the observation positions that can be used to observe particular parts of the archer's form. Note that not only are errors identified but space is provided for an accompanying correction. Students should use this chart both to identify their own errors and to identify ways to correct those errors. For example, if one shoulder is higher than the other, a student lists a correction on the chart: extend the bow arm straight to the target then draw back at shoulder level.

### ARROW PATTERN ANALYSIS

An arrow pattern analysis is easily done with little or no additional equipment. For this reason, it is used more often than a technique analysis via photographs or videotapes. Archers should be encouraged, however, to plot their arrow patterns on charts. It is easy to forget what pattern was formed on previous ends or previous days, and some patterns are slow to form. That is, an archer might shoot one arrow out of every ten off-center in the 3 o'clock position. A written record shows the archer that this error is repeated over time, rather than being only an isolated poor shot.

Archers should always be encouraged to match their errors with possible causes and the corrections for their flaws. The ''Arrow Pattern Analysis'' section in Step 8 of *Archery: Steps to Success* (pp. 69-81) lists the possible causes for errors along the major dimensions. For example, the causes of a high or 12 o'clock arrow are listed. Remind archers that errors in an oblique direction—for example, 10 o'clock— should be checked against the chart for the appropriate major dimensions, 12 o'clock and 9 o'clock. Single causes found in both lists can be suspected as likely for that oblique-direction error.

# Selected Activities
# for Analyzing Technique
# and Arrow Pattern Errors

## 1. Picture Analysis
## (Photograph)
[Corresponds to *Archery*, Step 8, Drill 2]

### Group Management and Safety Tips

- Students should pair up unless you will do all of the photography yourself.
- One target at the end of the practice range can be designated for photographing, and one archer photographed at a time, while the remainder of the class practices.
- Remind students to use the downrange observation position only when the archer is mimicking a shot without an arrow.

### Equipment

- Camera and film
- 1 Technique Analysis Chart and 1 clipboard for each student
- Standard archery tackle for every student
- An officiating stand, ladder, or chair for the above position

### Instructions to Class

- "Photographers, take at least one full-length photograph with the archer at full draw from each of the following positions: uprange, front, rear, and downrange. Take at least one close-up from each of the following positions: front, rear, and oblique. Take photographs of the follow-through from the front, rear, downrange, and oblique positions."
- "Archers, when your photographs are developed, fill out a Technique Analysis Chart from your photographs. Draw lines on the photographs to check for T-alignment and erect posture."
- "Be sure to include corrections for each of the errors identified on the chart."
- "Use the 'Technique Analysis' section in Step 8 of *Archery: Steps to Success* (pp. 81-85) for a review of common technique errors and corrections."

### Student Option

- "Take a photograph from the above position, also."

### Student Keys to Success

- Shoot as you have been
- Concentrate on each shot
- Forget about the camera
- Think only about aiming

### Student Success Goal

- Correctly identify technique errors from photographs

### To Reduce Difficulty

- Reduce the number of pictures to be taken.

### To Increase Difficulty

- Have student take additional close-up views.

## Technique Analysis Chart

Archer _____  Class _____  Date _____

Observation:  _____ Direct  _____ Videotape  _____ Photographs

Check "Yes" or "No." If "No," specify flaw and correction.

| Criterion | Observation position[a] | Yes | No | Technique flaw | Correction |
|---|---|---|---|---|---|
| *Stance* | | | | | |
| Straddles line | F, R | | | | |
| Weight even | F, R | | | | |
| Consistent | F, U | | | | |
| Stance aligned | U | | | | |
| Body erect | F, R | | | | |
| *Nock* | | | | | |
| Arrow placed correctly | O | | | | |
| Arrow against nock locator | O | | | | |
| *Bow hand and arm* | | | | | |
| Consistent hand position | O | | | | |
| Behind handle | O, A | | | | |
| Hand relaxed | O, R | | | | |
| Elbow rotated down | O | | | | |
| *Draw* | | | | | |
| Proper hook | O, F | | | | |
| Draw hand flat, relaxed | O, F | | | | |
| Elbow back first | F | | | | |
| Elbow at shoulder level | F, R | | | | |
| Shoulders level, aligned | F, U, A | | | | |
| *Anchor* | | | | | |
| Anchor positioned properly | F, O | | | | |
| Consistent anchor | F, O | | | | |
| Teeth together | F, O | | | | |
| Kisser button positioned | F, O | | | | |
| *Aim* | | | | | |
| Bow level | U, D | | | | |
| Correct eye | F, D | | | | |
| String aligned | U | | | | |
| Settles and holds | F, O | | | | |
| *Release* | | | | | |
| By relaxing hook | F, O, U | | | | |
| Head steady | U, A | | | | |
| Bow hand, arm steady | A, R | | | | |
| *Follow-through* | | | | | |
| Head steady | U, A | | | | |
| Bow arm up | F, R | | | | |
| Draw hand follows through | F, U, A | | | | |

[a]Observation positions: F = front, R = rear, U = uprange, D = downrange, O = oblique, A = above

Goals for next practice session: _____

_____

_____

Observer _____  Shooting distance _____  Conditions _____

# 2. Picture Analysis (Videotape)
[Corresponds to *Archery*, Step 8, Drill 2]

## Group Management and Safety Tips

- Students should pair up unless you will do all of the videotaping yourself.
- Designate an end target as the videotaping station.
- Videotape one archer at a time.
- Provide a backdrop with vertical and level horizontal lines.

## Equipment

- Video camera
- Backdrop with vertical and level horizontal lines
- 1 Technique Analysis Chart and 1 clipboard for each student
- Standard archery tackle for each student

## Instructions to Class

- ''Photographers, videotape the archer from each of the observation positions, zooming in on the anchor, draw hand, and bow hand where appropriate.''
- ''Archers, we will view your videotape together and identify any technique errors on a Technique Analysis Chart.''
- ''You should then complete the chart by identifying the corrections you should make.

- ''Use the 'Technique Analysis' section in Step 8 of *Archery: Steps to Success* (pp. 81-85) for a review of common technique errors and corrections.''
- ''Write out goals for your next practice session based on these corrections.''

## Student Option

- ''Provide your own videotape and be taped periodically.''

## Student Keys to Success

- Shoot as you have been
- Concentrate on each shot
- Forget about the camera
- Think only about aiming

## Student Success Goal

- Correctly identify technique errors from videotapes

## To Reduce Difficulty

- Your student could view the videotape in slow motion.

## To Increase Difficulty

- Your student should analyze the videotape on his or her own.

# Technique Analysis Chart

Archer _____ Class _____ Date _____

Observation: _____ Direct _____ Videotape _____ Photographs

Check "Yes" or "No." If "No," specify flaw and correction.

| Criterion | Observation position[a] | Yes | No | Technique flaw | Correction |
|---|---|---|---|---|---|
| *Stance* | | | | | |
| Straddles line | F, R | | | | |
| Weight even | F, R | | | | |
| Consistent | F, U | | | | |
| Stance aligned | U | | | | |
| Body erect | F, R | | | | |
| *Nock* | | | | | |
| Arrow placed correctly | O | | | | |
| Arrow against nock locator | O | | | | |
| *Bow hand and arm* | | | | | |
| Consistent hand position | O | | | | |
| Behind handle | O, A | | | | |
| Hand relaxed | O, R | | | | |
| Elbow rotated down | O | | | | |
| *Draw* | | | | | |
| Proper hook | O, F | | | | |
| Draw hand flat, relaxed | O, F | | | | |
| Elbow back first | F | | | | |
| Elbow at shoulder level | F, R | | | | |
| Shoulders level, aligned | F, U, A | | | | |
| *Anchor* | | | | | |
| Anchor positioned properly | F, O | | | | |
| Consistent anchor | F, O | | | | |
| Teeth together | F, O | | | | |
| Kisser button positioned | F, O | | | | |
| *Aim* | | | | | |
| Bow level | U, D | | | | |
| Correct eye | F, D | | | | |
| String aligned | U | | | | |
| Settles and holds | F, O | | | | |
| *Release* | | | | | |
| By relaxing hook | F, O, U | | | | |
| Head steady | U, A | | | | |
| Bow hand, arm steady | A, R | | | | |
| *Follow-through* | | | | | |
| Head steady | U, A | | | | |
| Bow arm up | F, R | | | | |
| Draw hand follows through | F, U, A | | | | |

[a]Observation positions: F = front, R = rear, U = uprange, D = downrange, O = oblique, A = above

Goals for next practice session: _____

_____

_____

Observer _____ Shooting distance _____ Conditions _____

# 3. Arrow Pattern Analysis
[Corresponds to *Archery*, Step 8, Drill 1]

## Group Management and Safety Tips

- A sample of the Arrow Pattern Analysis Chart is given to show how it might be filled out by your students.
- Distribute Arrow Pattern Analysis Charts to every student.
- Select a shooting distance.

## Equipment

- Standard archery tackle for every student
- 1 target butt, 1 target face, and bale pins for every four students
- 1 Arrow Pattern Analysis Chart and 1 clipboard for each student

## Instructions to Class

- "Shoot 6-arrow ends as you normally do but, before pulling your arrows from the target, plot their positions on the target face onto your chart with Xs."
- "Plot one end on each target chart."
- "At the end of our shooting session, analyze your arrow patterns. Analyze each end for directional error but also check for occasional arrows of the same directional error in different ends."
- "Use the 'Arrow Pattern Analysis' section in Step 8 of *Archery: Steps to Success* (pp. 69-81) to identify the possible causes of your directional errors. List the corrections for these possible causes. Make the corrections your goals for your next practice session."

## Student Option

- "Compare your arrow pattern analysis with your most recent technique analysis."

## Student Keys to Success

- Shoot as you have been
- Concentrate on each shot
- Think only about aiming

## Student Goal

- Correctly identify technique errors from arrow patterns

## To Reduce Difficulty

- Activity is already in its simplest form.

## To Increase Difficulty

- Have student shoot from a variety of distances.

## Sample Arrow Pattern Analysis Chart

Archer __Sample_____  Class __9:30 MW_____  Date __9/23/90___

Shooting distance __20 yds_____  Special conditions __new stance, slight_____

__left-to-right wind_____

Mark locations of arrows with Xs.

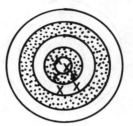 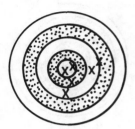  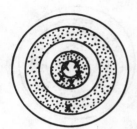

Error analysis:          Error analysis:          Error analysis:          Error analysis:

__6 o'clock_____    __6 o'clock, 3 o'clock__    __6 o'clock, 3 o'clock__    __6 o'clock (1 shot)__

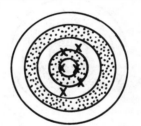 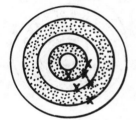 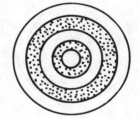 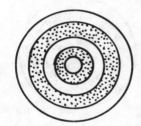

Error analysis:          Error analysis:          Error analysis:          Error analysis:

__12 o'clock, 6 o'clock__  __5 o'clock__

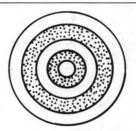 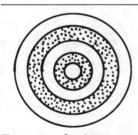 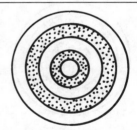 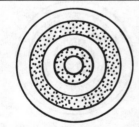

Error analysis:          Error analysis:          Error analysis:          Error analysis:

Possible causes of directional errors: __dropping bow arm, wind gusts, creeping, elevat-
ing bow shoulder, body lean__

Suggested corrections: __stand erect, draw with back muscle & maintain back tension,
extend bow arm to target in follow through__

Goals for next practice session: __To take an erect stance; To use good back tension;
To follow through to target__

# Arrow Pattern Analysis Chart

Archer _____ Class _____ Date _____

Shooting distance _____ Special conditions _____

_____

Mark locations of arrows with Xs.

Error analysis:

_____   _____   _____   _____
_____   _____   _____   _____

Error analysis:

_____   _____   _____   _____
_____   _____   _____   _____

Error analysis:

_____   _____   _____   _____
_____   _____   _____   _____

Possible causes of directional errors: _____

_____

Suggested corrections: _____

_____

Goals for next practice session: _____

_____

# Step 9  Varying the Stance

Varying the stance is the first in a series of technical basic form adaptations that the archer can make. Some of these are desirable variations considering the archer's body build, some capitalize on the archer's strength or flexibility, and others are simply a matter of preference. Your student should have the opportunity to experiment with these variations, but you as instructor must monitor him or her closely to see that he or she implements the variation correctly, can duplicate it over prolonged shooting periods, and can still maintain T-alignment.

The following chart allows you to rate students as they learn variations of the stance. A change in foot position is the most obvious difference among the stances, and most students can easily implement this change. You must develop a critical eye for the subtle differences in shooting position that accompany changes in stance. Most important among these is alignment with the target, even if the stance is open or closed. You must particularly rate this aspect of shooting and help beginners and intermediates learn to align their new stances.

## Stance Rating

| CRITERION | BEGINNING LEVEL | INTERMEDIATE LEVEL | ADVANCED LEVEL |
|---|---|---|---|
| **Square Stance** | • Distributes weight unevenly<br>• Places feet too close or far apart<br><br>• Does not align toes<br><br><br><br><br><br><br>• Fails to stand in front of target | • Distributes weight evenly<br>• Places feet shoulder width apart<br><br>• Aligns toes, but not along a line directly to bull's-eye, especially if shooting position is not directly in front of target | • Distributes weight evenly<br>• Places feet shoulder width apart<br><br>• Aligns toes along line to bull's-eye, even if slightly left or right of target |

## *Stance Rating*

| CRITERION | BEGINNING LEVEL | INTERMEDIATE LEVEL | ADVANCED LEVEL |
|---|---|---|---|
| **Open Stance** | • Distributes weight unevenly<br>• Aligns back foot only along line to bull's-eye<br><br>• Fails to square shoulders along a line to target<br>• Uses arm muscles more than back muscles to draw | • Distributes weight evenly<br>• Sometimes fails to line up along a line to bull's-eye<br><br>• Has upper body slightly open to target<br>• Has slightly too much tension in arm | • Distributes weight evenly<br>• Lines up along a line to target with middle of rear foot, toes of front foot on line<br>• Squares shoulders along a line to target<br>• Has good back tension |
| **Closed Stance** | • Distributes weight unevenly<br>• Tends to lean away from target<br>• Tends to overdraw<br><br>• Strikes clothing or bow arm if stance is too closed | • Distributes weight evenly<br>• Allows hips to shift toward target<br>• Anchors at proper position<br>• Tends to follow through to draw side | • Distributes weight evenly<br>• Stands erect<br><br>• Anchors at proper position<br>• Follows through straight to target |

# Error Detection and Correction for the Stances

As the novice archer begins to vary shooting form—adapting it to his or her body type, strength, and preference—he or she typically makes two kinds of errors. Obviously, your student can err in using the new variation. The archer could also unknowingly change the basic technique as a direct result of the new variation or because attention is diverted. This is an important time to watch for problems and correct them before they become habitual.

| ERROR | CORRECTION |
|---|---|
| 1. Archer leans away from target by laterally bending trunk, sometimes elevating front shoulder. 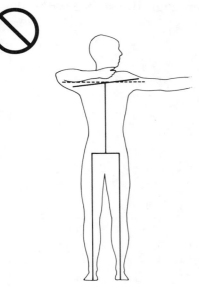 | 1. In taking a new stance the archer has varied from T-alignment. The new stance might be too extreme and should be slightly adjusted toward a square position. Weight should be even and posture erect, regardless of stance position. |
| 2. Shoulders are not aligned with target. 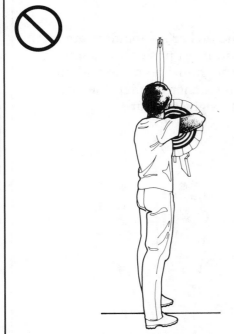 | 2. The archer is letting the shoulders follow the feet. Stand behind the archer, sighting down the shoulders to the target. *Before* the draw, remind archer to rotate the trunk to align the shoulders. Check the archer's alignment. |

**ERROR**

**CORRECTION**

3. An imaginary line through the archer's stance does not intersect the bull's-eye.

3. Have the archer use golf tees or chalk marks indoors and step away to check alignment, adjusting as necessary until he or she can align the stance without such aid.

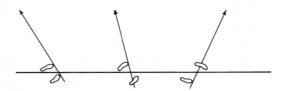

4. Head overrotates.

4. Be sure the archer's shoulders are aligned and head position is maintained throughout the draw and aim. Remind the archer to align the bowstring with sight aperture.

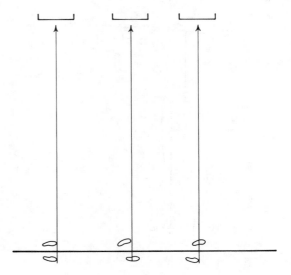

| ERROR 🚫 | CORRECTION |
|---|---|
| 5. Archer is inconsistent in assuming the stance. | 5. Open and closed stances are more difficult to duplicate, especially before they are well learned. Foot markers should be used. A rubber door mat can be used to more permanently mark and preserve the stance to be duplicated. |

# Selected Stance Drills

## 1. Impact Variation
[Corresponds to *Archery*, Step 9, Drill 1]

**Group Management and Safety Tips**
- Place students in a single line, three or four to a target.
- Have students shoot from the 20-yard line.
- Selectively watch students to see that they maintain upper-body alignment to the target as they vary their stances.

**Equipment**
- Standard archery tackle
- 1 target butt, 1 target face, and 4 bale pins for every four students

**Instructions to Class**
- "Experiment with varying degrees of open and closed stances."
- "Do not change your left-right sight setting (as long as arrows are on target butt) until you decide which stance is best for you."
- "Record in *Archery: Steps to Success* the average number of inches the middle of your arrow groups drift from the bull's-eye as you open and close your stance."
- "Decide which stance you will use, then check it with the Alignment Check drill (*Archery*, Step 9, Drill 2). Sketch the stance you decide upon."
- "Adjust your sight setting."

**Student Option**
- "Use differently colored golf tees (or colored chalk indoors) to mark variations of your stance."

**Student Keys to Success**
- Position feet in desired stance position
- Weight even
- Shoulders aligned to target
- Line to target intersects bull's-eye

**Student Success Goal**
- See the effect of varying the stance and choosing a stance that does not promote drift

**To Reduce Difficulty**
- Drill is already in its simplest form.

**To Increase Difficulty**
- Student should move on to the following drills.

# 2. Golf Tee Drill
[Corresponds to *Archery*, Step 9, Drill 3]

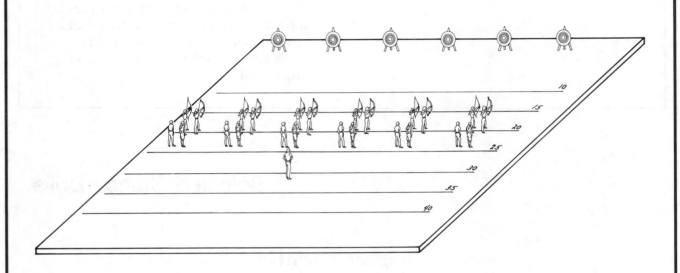

## Group Management and Safety Tips

- Have students pair up and go to a target.
- Distribute 2 golf tees to each student (chalk can substitute indoors).
- Students should shoot from the 20-yard line, with partners alternating.

## Equipment

- 2 golf tees per student (or chalk if indoors)
- Standard archery tackle, targets, and bale pins

## Instructions to Class

- "Alternate being a shooter and observer on successive ends."
- "Shooting partner, assume a stance and place your golf tees at your toes. Shoot an end while your observing partner examines your alignment to the target."
- "Before retrieving your arrows, check with your partner and decide whether or not an imaginary line through your stance (as indicated by the golf tees) intersected the target bull's-eye."
- "Shooting partner, shoot again, adjusting your stance, if necessary, with the help of your partner."

## Student Option

- "Repeat several feet up and down the shooting line."

## Student Keys to Success

- Position feet
- Weight even
- Shoulders aligned to target
- Line to target intersects bull's-eye

## Student Success Goal

- Assume a stance 3 times that is aligned with the target

## To Reduce Difficulty

- Drill is already in its simplest form

## To Increase Difficulty

- Have your student walk through a field archery course, assuming and aligning the stance on uneven terrain.

# 3. *Distance Drill*
[Corresponds to *Archery*, Step 9, Drill 5]

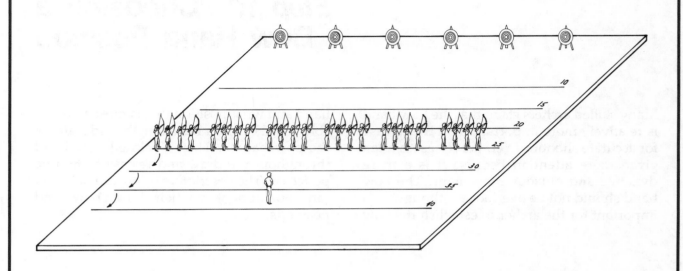

## Group Management and Safety Tips

- Have students shoot 6-arrow ends at 25, 30, 35, and 40 yards.
- Distribute 2 golf tees to each student.
- Selectively watch students by sighting downrange to check for stance alignment and shoulder alignment.

## Equipment

- Standard archery tackle and 2 golf tees for each student
- 1 target butt, 1 target face, and 4 bale pins for every four students

## Instructions to Class

- ''Use golf tees to mark your stance for shots at a specified distance.''
- ''Shoot 1 end each at 25, 30, 35, and 40 yards.''
- ''Plot your arrows on target charts.''
- ''After all your shooting is over, look for evidence that your alignment varied over distance by analyzing the left-right drift of your arrow groups.''

## Student Option

- ''Use the Alignment Check drill (*Archery*, Step 9, Drill 2) at each distance.''

## Student Keys to Success

- Straight line to bull's-eye intersects
  a. Toes in a square stance
  b. Approximately middle of rear foot and toes of front foot in open stance
  c. Toes of rear foot and approximately middle of front foot in closed stance

## Student Success Goal

- Maintain centering of arrow groups at increasing distances

## To Reduce Difficulty

- Drill is already in its simplest form.

## To Increase Difficulty

- Have student add ends at 45 and 50 yards.

# *Step 10*  Choosing a Bow Hand Position

Many skilled archers claim that the bow hand is relatively more important than the release for accurate shooting. Yet, the release is often given more attention because it is a more dynamic and obvious movement. The bow hand should not be overlooked, though. It is important for the archer to establish the bow hand and wrist position that is most comfortable, matches his or her strength, and matches the bow handle. Then a relaxed bow hand throughout the draw and release should be perfected. The descriptors below can help you rate your students on their chosen bow hand positions.

## *Bow Hand Position Rating*

| CRITERION | BEGINNING LEVEL | INTERMEDIATE LEVEL | ADVANCED LEVEL |
|---|---|---|---|
| Low Wrist | • Heels the bow on release<br><br>• Fails to center bow hand and arm behind center of bow<br><br>• Grips bow too tightly<br><br>• Holds bow too low on handle | • Holds wrist too stiffly<br><br>• Begins with relaxed hand, then grabs bow on release<br>• Tends to follow through to left (if right-handed)<br>• Holds bow at proper level on handle | • Places hand so that center of arm intersects center of bow<br>• Relaxes bow hand and fingers throughout shot<br><br>• Allows wrist to relax backward<br><br>• Holds bow at proper level on handle |

## Bow Hand Position Rating

| CRITERION | BEGINNING LEVEL | INTERMEDIATE LEVEL | ADVANCED LEVEL |
|---|---|---|---|
| High Wrist | • Tends to stiffen fingers<br><br>• Tends to grab bow on release<br><br>• Centers pressure on thumb | • With fatigue, tends to move wrist on release | • Maintains a relaxed hand and wrist<br><br>• Centers pressure on bow hand and arm |
| Straight Wrist | • Tends to stiffen fingers<br><br><br>• Centers pressure on thumb<br>• Holds bow too low on handle<br><br>• Tends to grab bow on release | • Centers pressure on skin web between thumb and forefinger, but wraps fingers around handle | • Notes deviations from shot to shot<br><br><br>• Centers pressure on skin web<br>• Maintains a relaxed hand and wrist<br>• Follows through straight to target |

## Error Detection and Correction for the Bow Hand Position

A skilled archer can demonstrate the importance of a consistent, relaxed bow hand position by varying the position just slightly on successive shots and producing a spread of arrows across the target. Below are bow hand position errors that have not been mentioned previously. Look for these errors in your students and offer the appropriate corrections. It is helpful to videotape the bow hand at release because of the quickness of any movement that might occur. Archers often overlook movements because they occur so quickly.

**ERROR**            **CORRECTION**

1. Archer does not have the bow hand and arm centered behind the bow.

1. Have the archer take the bow hand position and extend the bow arm without drawing. Grab the student's bow above and below the bow handle and push it lightly toward the archer. The student will feel the wrist break (flex or hyperextend) if the bow is not centered. Have the student adjust and repeat until the proper position is achieved. Help the student mark this position with stickers.

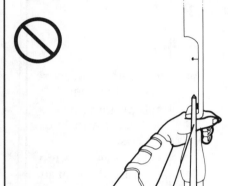

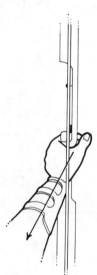

2. Archer tightly extends bow hand fingers to keep from gripping the bow.

2. This is self-defeating because the tension in the hand may lead the archer to grab the bow at release anyway. Have the archer relax the fingers before the draw and wiggle them to check for relaxation at full draw.

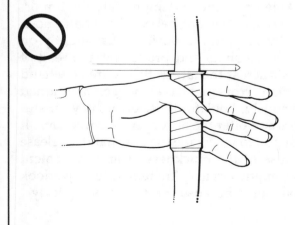

3. Archer breaks (flexes or hyperextends) wrist on release.

3. Fatigue may cause this. Changing to a low wrist position should be considered.

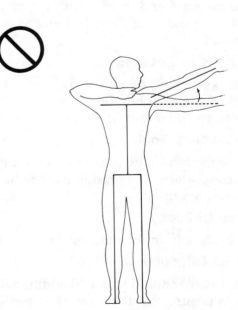

4. Archer heels the bow or jerks the bow arm up at release.

4. This may occur when the archer feels the bow arm dropping or is aiming low at release. Emphasize concentration on aiming at the middle of the bull's-eye so that such corrections will not be necessary.

| **ERROR** | **CORRECTION** |
|---|---|
| 5. Archer's hand slides on the bow handle during the aim and hold. | 5. This is probably caused by perspiration. The archer should keep a towel nearby to dry the hand and bow handle or use a drying powder. A bow handle "saddle," a piece of suede leather, also can be purchased to provide a better grip. |
| 6. Archer is inconsistent in establishing bow hand position on the handle. | 6. It is helpful to mark the bow handle with a sticker or marker line and match this indicator with an anatomical feature of the hand. Also, a special piece of leather with a sewn ridge can be purchased to mount on the bow handle so this ridge can be matched by feel to the hand position. Care must be taken in hot weather that the adhesive on this piece does not loosen. |

# Selected Bow Hand Position Drills

## 1. *Choosing a Bow Hand Position*
[Corresponds to *Archery*, Step 10, Drill 1]

**Group Management and Safety Tips**

- Place students in a single line, in groups of four.
- Have students shoot 6-arrow ends from 20 yards.
- Selectively assist students.

**Equipment**

- Standard archery tackle with a bow sling for each student
- 1 target butt, 1 target face, and 4 bale pins for every four students

**Instructions to Class**

- "From 20 yards, shoot 2 ends with each bow hand position—low wrist, straight wrist, and high wrist."
- "Do not change your sight setting until you decide on a bow hand position."
- "Note the comfort of the position and the tightness of the arrow group after each end."

**Student Option**

- "Add an extra end or two with a given bow hand position if there is doubt as to the results."

**Student Keys to Success**

- Center your bow hand arm behind the center of the bow handle
- Relax your hand and fingers

**Student Success Goal**

- Choose the bow hand position that is the most comfortable and produces the tightest arrow groups

**To Reduce Difficulty**

- Drill is already in its simplest form.

**To Increase Difficulty**

- Your student should shoot 10 additional ends to ensure that the bow hand position can be maintained even with fatigue.

## 2. *Torque Check*
[Corresponds to *Archery*, Step 10, Drill 3]

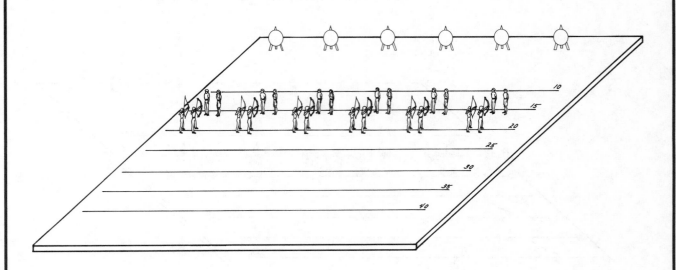

### Group Management and Safety Tips

- Have students pair up.
- Arrows should be kept in their quivers throughout this drill.
- Students should stand along a designated line when mimicking.

### Equipment

- Bows and finger tabs for every student

### Instructions to Class

- "Alternate mimicking a shot and observing your partner."
- "Observers, take a position a few feet downrange."
- "Archers, assume your stance and chosen bow hand position. Draw as you normally do."
- "Observers, note whether the back of the bow faces you, turns right, or turns left during the draw. If it turns, instruct the archer to adjust the bow hand position slightly (probably in the left-right direction)."
- "Repeat until you have each drawn 5 times in a row without torquing the bow."

### Student Option

- "Use a bow sling."

### Student Key to Success

- Keep the bow hand relaxed

### Student Success Goal

- 5 successive draws without torquing the bow

### To Reduce Difficulty

- Drill is already in its simplest form.

### To Increase Difficulty

- Have someone check for torque periodically during an extended shooting session (remembering to step back from the shooting line if others are shooting).

## 3. *Distance Practice*
[Corresponds to *Archery*, Step 10, Drill 5]

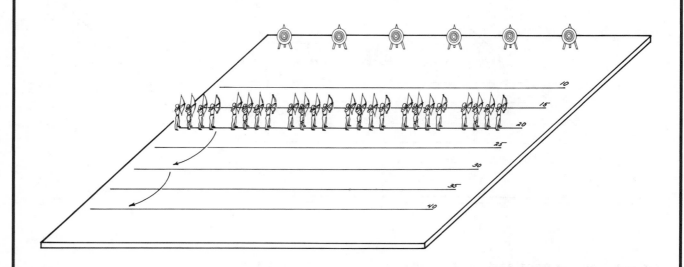

### Group Management and Safety Tips

- Assign 3 or 4 students to a target.
- Students will shoot from 20, 30, and 40 yards.
- Selectively watch students or videotape their bow hands.

### Equipment

- Standard archery tackle for every student
- 1 target butt, an 80-cm 10-ring target face, and bale pins for each 3- or 4-student group

### Instructions to Class

- "Shoot 3 six-arrow ends each at 20, 30, and 40 yards."
- "Plot your arrows on target charts. Analyze your directional errors for possible flaws in your bow hand technique."

### Student Option

- "Correct any bow hand errors evident after shooting at 30 yards before moving on to 40 yards."

### Student Keys to Success

- Keep your bow hand relaxed
- Keep your bow arm up to follow through

### Student Success Goal

- Accurate ends (no directional error) despite increasing shooting distance

### To Reduce Difficulty

- Your student should change distances after only one end.

### To Increase Difficulty

- Your student should correct any bow hand errors and repeat the drill.

# Step 11 Selecting an Anchor Position

Changing one's anchor position is a major adjustment in shooting form. When a student's body structure or interest in a type of archery dictates that another anchor position is preferred, it is helpful to the student to make the transition when you are available to observe and critique the form. You need to develop a critical eye for assessing all three of the anchor positions. The chart below gives the characteristics of beginning, intermediate, and advanced execution of all three anchor positions.

## Anchor Position Rating

| CRITERION | BEGINNING LEVEL | INTERMEDIATE LEVEL | ADVANCED LEVEL |
|---|---|---|---|
| Under-Chin Anchor | • Moves head forward to meet string<br>• Lets draw hand float beneath jaw<br>• Opens jaw<br><br>• Has kisser button out of position<br>• Fails to bring string all the way to touch chin and nose | • Touches string with chin or nose, but not both, or<br>• Lets string slide around side of nose and chin<br>• Has draw hand in in contact with jaw<br><br>• Has teeth together and kisser button between lips<br>• Tends to creep | • Touches string to middle of chin and nose<br>• Has draw hand in contact with jaw<br>• Has teeth together and kisser button between lips<br>• Relaxes draw hand, keeping back of hand flat |

## Anchor Position Rating

| CRITERION | BEGINNING LEVEL | INTERMEDIATE LEVEL | ADVANCED LEVEL |
|---|---|---|---|
| Side Anchor | • Tends to overdraw<br><br>• Tends to turn head to draw side<br><br>• Puts string on side of nose<br>• Draws string out, then in to face<br><br><br>• Has kisser button out of position<br><br>• Opens mouth when anchoring forefinger | • Tends to creep<br><br>• Tends to turn draw hand palm-down and torque string<br>• Touches string to front of nose<br>• Draws string straight back to face<br><br>• Places forefinger or kisser button in corner of mouth<br>• Occasionally opens mouth when anchoring fore-finger | • Keeps draw hand vertical<br>• Draws string straight back to face<br>• Touches string to front of nose<br>• Places forefinger or kisser button in corner of mouth<br><br>• Relaxes draw hand, keeping back of hand flat |
| Behind-Neck Anchor | • Places thumb high on neck or behind ear<br>• Turns draw hand palm-down and holds it away from neck<br>• Places string on side of nose, against cheek<br>• Has kisser button out of position | • Places thumb low on neck<br><br>• Turns draw hand palm-down<br><br><br>• Touches string to front of nose and side of chin<br>• Places kisser button between lips<br>• Draws slightly out, then brings hand in to neck | • Places thumb low on neck<br><br>• Keeps draw hand vertical and against neck<br><br>• Touches string to front of nose and side of chin<br>• Places kisser button between lips<br>• Draws straight back<br><br>• Relaxes draw hand, keeping back of hand flat |

# Error Detection and Correction for the Anchor Position

Any time an archer changes technique, there is the potential for form flaws to develop, even flaws not previously experienced or connected directly to the change. This is an important time to monitor form. Problems with the anchor and release were identified in several earlier steps. Those given below are very common anchor and release problems not mentioned previously.

**ERROR**

**CORRECTION**

1. Plucking occurs.

1. The archer probably has more tension than desirable in the arm and hand. Cue the archer to relax the arm and hand at the beginning of the draw, and to do the work by moving the elbow back. The archer might be trying to force the release to happen, rather than merely relaxing the hook.

**ERROR**

**CORRECTION**

2. Creeping occurs.

2. The archer is failing to maintain back tension until release. Encourage the archer to increase back tension while aiming. Use of a clicker requires an increase in back tension.

3. The draw hand torques the string.

3. The archer is probably turning the draw hand slightly palm-down. Be sure the hand is straight up and down when the hook is set and kept in this position during the draw, anchor, and hold. In a behind-neck anchor, the little finger should be felt against the neck. Some archers point their little fingers down and place them on their necks, chests, or even bowstrings; the archer must take care not to develop too much tension in the draw hand with these methods, though.

**ERROR**

**CORRECTION**

4. Archer varies the length of the draw (this can be detected by where the arrow stops on the arrow rest).

4. The archer might be moving the head toward or away from the target, before or during the draw and anchor, or rotating the head to the draw side during the anchor and hold. Encourage the archer to stand erect before the draw, then to move the hand to the anchor. A clicker or other draw check also guarantees that the arrow is drawn the same length on every shot.

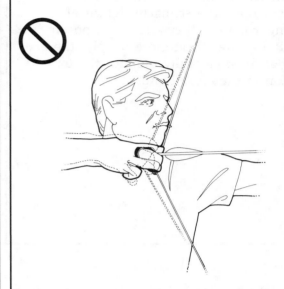

5. Archer with a compound bow finds the fingers are squeezed together, sometimes squeezing the arrow nock.

5. The shorter tip-to-tip length of a compound bow results in a more acute string angle at full draw. Your student might find that this results in an uncomfortable draw hand, especially if he or she has a large hand or a short-limbed bow. A two-finger hook can be considered, with usually the second and ring fingers (sometimes the forefinger and second finger) placed below the arrow. Your student should take care to keep the back of the hand flat and relaxed.

6. Archer using a clicker curls draw fingers to go through the clicker.

6. This is common when the archer becomes fatigued. Encourage the archer merely to form the hook, keeping the rest of the draw hand relaxed from the very start of the draw, using the back muscles for the draw. Conditioning through practice or strength training is beneficial for overcoming this problem.

**ERROR**

**CORRECTION**

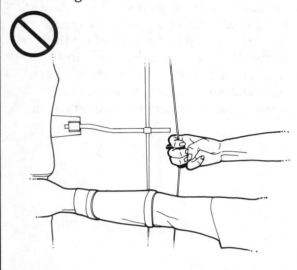

7. Student holds the string too deeply on the fingers.

7. Some archers shoot successfully with this method, but it often leads to flexion of the base knuckles or increased tension in the hand. Have your student place the string in the distal finger joint. Otherwise, if purposely placing the string more deeply, the archer must carefully monitor the tension in the draw hand.

# Selected Anchor Position Drills

## 1. *Mimic With Eyes Closed*
[Corresponds to *Archery*, Step 11, Drill 2]

**Group Management and Safety Tips**
- Archers should take a stance on a designated line, in groups of four.
- Arrows should be kept in quivers throughout this drill.

**Equipment**
- Bow and finger tab for each student

**Instructions to Class**
- "Assume your stance, bow hand grip, and hook."
- "Raise the bow, close your eyes, and draw to your under-chin anchor. Feel for the right position, count to 3, then ease the string back."
- "Draw 9 more times."
- "Repeat all this with the side anchor and behind-neck anchor."

**Student Option**
- None

**Student Keys to Success**
- Draw close to bow arm
- Touch kisser button
- Feel string on nose and chin
- Relax back of hand

**Student Success Goal**
- 10 successive correct anchors at each anchor position

**To Reduce Difficulty**
- Drill is already in its simplest form.

**To Increase Difficulty**
- Student should proceed to the following drills.

# 2. Setting the Kisser Button
[Corresponds to *Archery*, Step 11, Drill 3]

### Group Management and Safety Tips

- Have students pair up, alternately setting their kisser buttons.
- Each student should slip a kisser button onto the bowstring above the nock locator.

### Equipment

- A bow equipped with a kisser button for each student

### Instructions to Class

- "Take a normal stance and draw to the anchor position you plan to use."
- "Partners, slide the kisser button up or down until it is positioned between the archer's lips."
- "Mark this location on the bowstring with a felt marker."

### Student Option

- "Set the kisser button alone by alternately anchoring and adjusting the button."

### Student Key to Success

- Touch kisser button to mouth

### Student Success Goal

- Correctly position the kisser button

### To Reduce Difficulty

- Drill is already in its simplest form.

### To Increase Difficulty

- Student should proceed to the following drills.

## 3. *Guided Blind Shoot*
[Corresponds to *Archery*, Step 11, Drill 4]

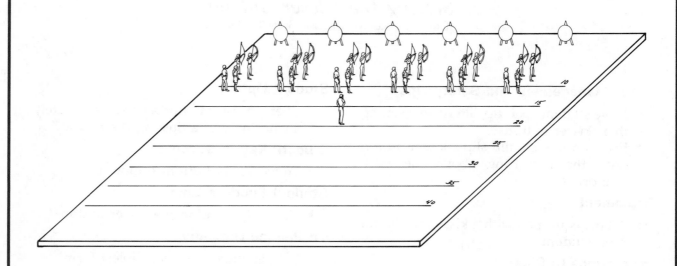

### Group Management and Safety Tips

- Have students pair up, alternately shooting and guiding.
- Students should not shoot from a distance greater than 7 yards.
- Remind students to release only after the cues from their partners.

### Equipment

- Standard archery tackle for every student
- 1 target butt for every four students

### Instructions to Class

- ''Shooter, take your stance, set your hands, close your eyes, and draw. Feel for the correct anchor position.''
- ''Partner, stand behind the archer and check the height of the bow arm. Tell the shooter to raise or lower the bow arm to assure a hit on the target. When the arm is positioned, say 'Okay.' ''
- ''Shooter, release when you hear your partner say 'Okay.' ''

### Student Option

- None

### Student Keys to Success

- Touch the kisser button to lips
- Feel string on nose and chin
- Relax the back of the draw hand
- Relax the hook to release

### Student Success Goal

- 10 blind shots with clean releases

### To Reduce Difficulty

- Drill is already in its simplest form.

### To Increase Difficulty

- Student should proceed to the following drills.

# 4. *Sight-Setting Drill*

[Corresponds to *Archery*, Step 11, Drill 5]

## Group Management and Safety Tips

- Place students in a single line, in groups of four.
- Students should shoot from 10, 15, 20, 25, 30, 35, and 40 yards.
- The entire class should shoot from the same distance at the same time.

## Equipment

- Standard archery tackle for every student
- 1 target butt, 1 target face, and bale pins for every four students

## Instructions to Class

- ''Reestablish your sight settings with your new or perfected anchor. Start with your old sight setting for 10 yards and adjust it as indicated by the directional error of your shots.''
- ''Shoot 2 six-arrow ends at each distance.''
- ''At subsequent distances start with your old settings and adjust them the same amount and direction as with the previous distance.''
- ''Record your new sight settings.''

## Student Option

- ''Obtain sight settings for 10, 20, 30, and 40 yards and interpolate the settings for 15, 25, and 35 yards.''

## Student Keys to Success

- Anchor consistently
- Aim
- Follow through

## Student Success Goal

- Obtain an accurate sight setting at each distance

## To Reduce Difficulty

- Drill is already in its simplest form.

## To Increase Difficulty

- Have your student also obtain settings for 45 and 50 yards.

# 5. Arrow Pattern Check
[Corresponds to *Archery*, Step 11, Drill 6]

## Group Management and Safety Tips

- Place students in a single line, in groups of four.
- Students should shoot from 20 yards.
- Distribute Arrow Analysis Charts or have students use the small targets in *Archery: Steps to Success*, Step 11, Drill 6.

## Equipment

- Standard archery tackle for every student
- 1 target butt, 1 target face, and bale pins for every four students
- Arrow Pattern Analysis Charts for each student or have students bring the participant's book

## Instructions to Class

- "Shoot 2 six-arrow ends, plotting your directional errors on a target chart."
- "Identify your errors, their possible causes, and how you can correct them. Focus on errors related to anchoring."
- "Shoot 2 additional ends to check for improvement."

## Student Option

- "Correct any directional errors after each end."

## Student Keys to Success

- Touch the kisser button to your lips
- Touch the bowstring to your chin and nose
- Aim
- Relax to release
- Follow through

## Student Success Goal

- 12 shots without the directional errors identified in previous ends

## To Reduce Difficulty

- Your student could shoot from only 15 yards.

## To Increase Difficulty

- Your student should shoot from a longer distance.

# Arrow Pattern Analysis Chart

Archer _____ Class _____ Date _____

Shooting distance _____ Special conditions _____
_____

Mark locations of arrows with Xs.

Error analysis:      Error analysis:      Error analysis:      Error analysis:

_____   _____   _____   _____

_____   _____   _____   _____

Error analysis:      Error analysis:      Error analysis:      Error analysis:

_____   _____   _____   _____

_____   _____   _____   _____

Error analysis:      Error analysis:      Error analysis:      Error analysis:

_____   _____   _____   _____

_____   _____   _____   _____

Possible causes of directional errors: _____
_____

Suggested corrections: _____
_____

Goals for next practice session: _____
_____

## 6. *Video Check*
[Corresponds to *Archery*, Step 11, Drill 7]

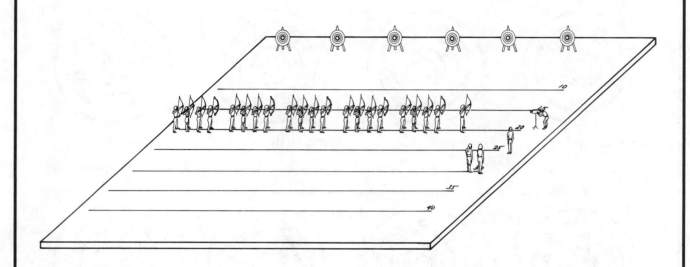

### Group Management and Safety Tips

- Designate an end target as a videotaping station.
- Students should rotate to the videotaping station as others practice.
- All students should shoot from the same selected distance.

### Equipment

- Standard archery tackle for every student
- 1 target butt, 1 target face, and bale pins
- Video camera

### Instructions to Class

- "Archer, shoot 2 six-arrow ends."
- "Photographer, film the anchor and release close up from both the front and oblique positions."
- "Archer, review your videotape, looking for consistency in your anchor position over the 12 shots, as well as for proper execution."

### Student Option

- "Videotape shooting with a second anchor position."

### Student Keys to Success

- Draw smoothly to your anchor
- Feel the kisser button and string
- Aim
- Relax the hook to release
- Follow through

### Student Success Goal

- 12 shots with a consistent anchor

### To Reduce Difficulty

- Have student review the videotape with your assistance.

### To Increase Difficulty

- Have your student videotape his or her anchor position periodically, keeping all videotape results on the same videocassette.

# 7. *Scoring Drill*

[Corresponds to *Archery*, Step 11, Drill 8]

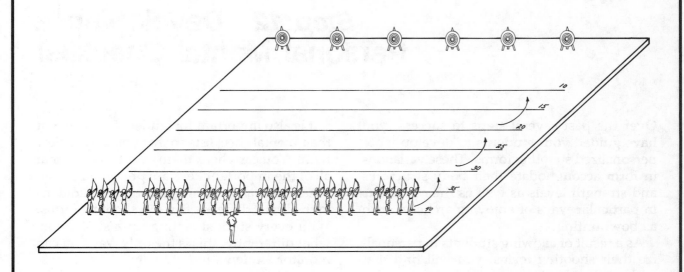

## Group Management and Safety Tips

- Have the class start at 40 yards, moving to 30, 20, and 10 yards.
- The class shoots 4 six-arrow ends at each distance.

## Equipment

- Standard archery tackle for every student
- 1 target butt, an 80-cm target face, and bale pins for every four students
- 1 scorecard per student
- Extra copies of the Arrow Pattern Analysis Chart

## Instructions to Class

- "Shoot 4 ends of 6 arrows at each distance."
- "Score and record each of your ends, using 10-ring scoring."

## Student Option

- "Chart shots on an Arrow Pattern Analysis Chart, as well as keep score."

## Student Keys to Success

- Draw smoothly
- Anchor consistently
- Aim
- Follow through

## Student Success Goal

- Improve your score at each successive distance

## To Reduce Difficulty

- Have your student shoot from the 3 shortest distances only.

## To Increase Difficulty

- Make your student shoot at a 60-cm face from 20 and 10 yards.

# Step 12 Developing a Personal Mental Checklist

Over the past several steps to success, you have guided your students to develop more personalized shooting forms. These variations in form accommodate their body structures and strength levels as well as their interests in particular ways of enjoying archery, such as bowhunting.

As a result of allowing students to personalize their shooting forms, you will find that each student begins to use his or her own list of keys or personal mental checklist to set up a shot. Each student sets up the shot a little differently. In addition, each probably has one or two reminders to help overcome a shooting flaw.

It is important to have beginning archers write out their personal lists of keys. This is because many students overlook the importance of setting up each and every shot in exactly the same way. Having become aware of possible variations in stance, bow hand position, and anchor position, they may mistakenly assume these can vary from shot to shot, or they may simply not attend to keeping them consistent from shot to shot. Writing out their own checklists helps them consolidate their personal concepts of setting up shots and emphasizes the procedures for following these concepts on each and every shot.

It is also important for students to write out their mental checklists so that you may review them. You can check them over to assure that all of the important keys are present. You can observe the archers, and can suggest additions to the lists if there are flaws in shooting forms. With every student setting up a shot somewhat differently, this is the only way you can monitor students individually.

A master sheet for duplicating checklist forms is included in Drill 1. It is arranged in a narrow format so that each student may tape a copy to his or her lower bow limb. The form also includes some prompts to remind students of important keys that should be included in their personal lists. The first activity drill in this step incorporates the personal mental checklist.

This is an important time to give students ample practice with their new, personalized forms. Many practice activities are suggested, allowing students to firmly establish their updated shot preparations. Use of the personalized checklist is carried over into many of these practice activities.

# Selected Personal Mental Checklist Drills

## 1. *Learning Your Checklist*
[Corresponds to *Archery*, Step 12, Drills 1 and 2]

### Group Management and Safety Tips

- Using the master Personal Checklist sheets provided in this drill, make a duplicate checklist for each shooter, preferably on heavy paper or card stock.
- Distribute a blank checklist to each shooter.

### Equipment

- Personal Checklists (p. 108) for every archer
- Tape
- Standard archery tackle for every archer
- 1 target butt with an 80-cm target face for every four shooters

### Instructions to Class

- "Write your personal checklist on the form provided."
- "Consult the Keys to Success in Steps 9, 10, and 11 of *Archery: Steps to Success* to determine the keys for the variations you have chosen in stance, bow hand position, and anchor position. Include keys to correct any flaws that have been a problem for you."
- "After I review your checklist, tape it to the bottom limb of your bow."
- "Shoot 4 ends at 20 yards, reciting the steps in your checklist as you prepare your shots. Recite aloud the keys up to anchoring, then say the remaining keys silently."

### Student Option

- "Memorize the checklist before shooting."

### Student Keys to Success

- Follow your checklist
- Prepare each shot identically

### Student Success Goal

- Execute each item in the personal checklist while shooting all arrows

### To Reduce Difficulty

- Have your student shoot at a 122-cm target.
- Have a partner read the archer's checklist as he or she shoots arrows in the first end.

### To Increase Difficulty

- Make the archer shoot from a longer distance.
- Have your student change distances on every end.

## Personal Checklist

Name _____   Class _____

Stance _____

Grip _____

Hook _____

Draw _____

Anchor _____

Alignment _____

Aiming _____

Release _____

Follow-through _____

## Personal Checklist

Name _____   Class _____

Stance _____

Grip _____

Hook _____

Draw _____

Anchor _____

Alignment _____

Aiming _____

Release _____

Follow-through _____

## Personal Checklist

Name _____   Class _____

Stance _____

Grip _____

Hook _____

Draw _____

Anchor _____

Alignment _____

Aiming _____

Release _____

Follow-through _____

## 2. *Balloon Practice*
[Corresponds to *Archery*, Step 12, Drill 3]

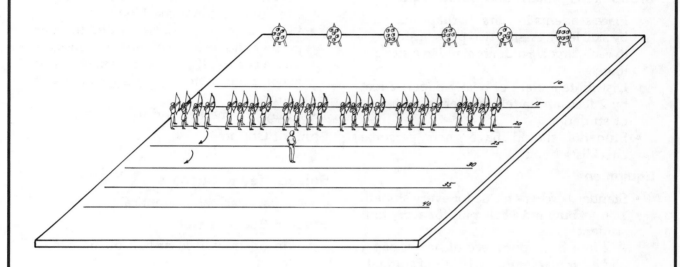

### Group Management and Safety Tips

- Place students in groups of four and assign each group to a target. Students should stand in a straight line.
- Distribute balloons.
- Students should have their personal mental checklists handy.

### Equipment

- Standard archery tackle for every student
- 1 target butt for every four students
- 24 balloons for every four students

### Instructions to Class

- "In groups of four, tape 6 balloons to your target butt."
- "Shoot from 20 yards, using your personal mental checklist. Try to break all of the balloons on one end."
- "Repeat at 25 and 30 yards."

### Student Option

- "Recite aloud the keys up to anchoring."

### Student Key to Success

- Prepare each shot identically

### Student Success Goal

- Break all the balloons on the target butt in 1 end

### To Reduce Difficulty

- Let student use large balloons.

### To Increase Difficulty

- Make your student shoot from 25, 30, and 35 yards.

# 3. *Tic-Tac-Toe*
[Corresponds to *Archery*, Step 12, Drill 4]

## Group Management and Safety Tips

- Place students in pairs, perhaps matched by skill level. Assign two pairs of students to each target. Students stand in a straight line.
- Distribute a piece of heavy paper, 2 feet by 2 feet, and a felt marker to each pair of students.
- Students should have their personal checklists handy.

## Equipment

- Standard archery tackle for every student
- 1 target butt and 4 bale pins for every four students
- A 2-foot by 2-foot piece of heavy paper and a felt marker for each pair of students

## Instructions to Class

- ''Each pair of students, draw a tic-tac-toe pattern on your paper.''
- ''Combine with the other pair at your target to mount your papers one above the other on the target butt.''
- ''Flip a coin with your partner to determine who shoots first. Alternately take shots to play tic-tac-toe. A shot counts as taking a box if it lands inside a box on your paper without touching a line.''
- ''Shoot from 20 yards, remembering to use your personal checklist.''
- ''Give a copy of your checklist to your partner and recite all of the steps possible on every shot. If your partner catches you leaving out a step, your shot does not count.''
- ''Play 1 game per end for 6 ends.''

## Student Option

- None

## Student Key to Success

- Prepare each shot identically

## Student Success Goal

- Win or draw at least half of the games played

## To Reduce Difficulty

- Drill is already in its easiest form.

## To Increase Difficulty

- Have archer draw the tic-tac-toe pattern smaller.
- On ends 4, 5, and 6, have students move back to 25, 30, and 35 yards, respectively.

# 4. Subtract an Arrow
## [Corresponds to *Archery*, Step 12, Drill 5]

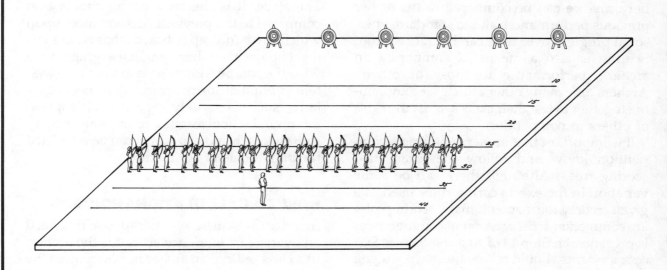

## Group Management and Safety Tips

- Place students in pairs, perhaps matched by skill level. Assign two pairs of students to each target.
- Place a roll of tape at each target.

## Equipment

- Standard archery tackle for every student
- 1 target butt, an 80-cm target face, and 1 roll of tape for every four students

## Instructions to Class

- "Wrap a piece of tape around one of your arrows, just in front of the fletching."
- "Shoot 5 unmarked arrows from 30 yards."
- "Before you take turns shooting your marked arrows, recite your personal mental checklist aloud, and have your partner check you."
- "If you recite your checklist correctly, shoot your marked arrow. When you score, subtract its value from your partner's score rather than count it toward your own score."
- "Shoot a total of 6 ends."

## Student Option

- None

## Student Keys to Success

- Prepare your shot carefully
- Follow through

## Student Success Goal

- Win half of the ends shot

## To Reduce Difficulty

- Let your student shoot from 25 yards.

## To Increase Difficulty

- Have your student shoot at a 60-cm target face.

# Step 13  Scoring

Scoring provides a means of evaluating archery performance. Through scoring, an archer's performance can be compared to his or her previous performances and to standards; personal progress over time can be tracked, too. Scoring is also a means of comparing an archer's performance to those of others. Archers, like many other athletes, enjoy coming together to test their skills against the skills of others in competition.

It is important that archers entering a competition know and follow the established scoring rules. Although there can be some variation in the exact scoring rules used in a given archery tournament, many scoring rules are common in archery. A set of common rules is presented in Step 13 of *Archery: Steps to Success*; students should follow these rules if you direct them to complete the practice activity presented later in this step.

People of various ages, sizes, strengths, abilities and disabilities, and of both sexes can all compete in archery. Archers often decide that a test of skill, a competition, is best if limited to archers similar in one or more of these factors. Equipment styles can also provide classifications for competition. Modern technology has also provided much variation in the types of archery equipment used today; an archer can shoot a recurve or compound bow, with a bowsight or without, holding the bowstring with their fingers or a mechanical release, and so on.

Though a consideration of the personal and equipment differences of archers is often appropriate, it is also desirable to provide settings where groups of archers who vary in these factors, such as family or school club members, can all compete together. A useful means by which this can be done is by handicapping scores.

A *handicap* is a means of equating archers who vary in personal or equipment classifications. An archer who scores low in absolute terms because of the equipment used, skill level, age, and so on, is given bonus points. Therefore, it is the archer who shoots best compared to the previous performances upon which the handicap is based (that is, the farthest above his or her personal average) who wins the competition. The handicapping system is popular for programs that meet regularly, such as weekly recreational leagues, intramural school leagues, or monthly archery club shoots. Handicap scores can be calculated for individuals or for teams.

## HOW TO CALCULATE HANDICAPS

In order to calculate a handicap, you first need an average or reference score for the archer. In a class setting, an archer needs to shoot the designated type of round at least once for a score before the handicapped event using the same round. In the case of a regular league or intramural program, an archer can establish a handicap at the first meeting. Thereafter, the handicap can be based on recent performances or on the average from, for example, the last two meetings or the entire series of previous meetings. Whenever possible, handicaps should be based on an average of two or more performances, in order to decrease the likelihood that the handicap is based on a single unusually high or low score for the archer.

The general method for calculating the handicap score for an event is to subtract an archer's reference score from the total possible number of points for that archery round. This difference can be the handicap, the number of points given to the archer in a subsequent event and added to the actual score shot in that event. Alternatively, a percentage of the difference can be calculated and used as the handicap; a popular percentage is 80%. This score is then added to the actual score shot in a subsequent event. Several examples follow.

### Example 1: The 100% Handicap, Individual

1. Suppose two archers shot the following scores on a round with a possible (perfect) score of 600:

|  | Archer A | Archer B |
|---|---|---|
| October 1 | 503 | 544 |
| October 8 | 534 | 550 |
| October 15 | 534 | 545 |

2. Calculate each archer's average over the first two weeks.

|  | Archer A | Archer B |
|---|---|---|
| Total, Week 1 + Week 2 | 1,037 | 1,094 |
| Average, Weeks 1 + 2 | 519 | 547 |
| Difference between average and 600 | 81 | 53 |

Note that fractions of 1/2 or more are rounded upward.

3. Add the difference (handicap) to the subsequent score.

|  | Archer A | Archer B |
|---|---|---|
| October 15 score | 534 | 545 |
| Handicap | 81 | 53 |
| Total | 615 | 598 |

Between the two archers, Archer A did better in the handicap event, even though Archer B shot a higher raw score. Note that Archer A's handicap score is actually higher than the total possible score for the round. Some programs cut off handicap scores at the total possible score, in this case 600. This allows the superior archer who shoots a perfect score without the benefit of a handicap to at least tie the handicap score of someone like Archer A.

### Example 2: 80% Handicap, Individual

1. Suppose you prefer the handicap to be 80% of the difference between the average and 600. For the archers above, calculate 80% of the differences between their averages and 600.

|  | Archer A | Archer B |
|---|---|---|
| Difference | 81 | 53 |
| 80% of difference | 65 | 42 |

2. Add the handicap to the subsequent score.

|  | Archer A | Archer B |
|---|---|---|
| October 15 score | 534 | 545 |
| Handicap | 65 | 42 |
| Total | 599 | 587 |

Note that Archer A still shot the higher handicap score, but the two scores are much closer. An 80% handicap gives a slight advantage to archers who shoot higher scores, compared to the 100% handicap, because archers must make up the remaining 20%. This is a larger number of points for archers with lower averages and, consequently, higher handicaps. On the other hand, they have more room for improvement and can perhaps make up those points easier than archers who have already neared the top of their games.

### Example 3: 80% Handicap, Team

1. Archery league competitions are often shot in a team format wherein the teams receive handicaps. Suppose the round shot in this example is 3 "games" of 10 arrows each on a 10-ring target for a total possible game score of 100. First calculate a current average for each archer by totaling his or her 6 previous games and dividing by 6. These averages are recorded for each archer on a team; then a team average is calculated.

| *Team A* | | *Team B* | |
|---|---|---|---|
| *Archer* | *Average* | *Archer* | *Average* |
| Jane | 92 | Tim | 87 |
| Joe | 87 | Theresa | 76 |
| Jennifer | 80 | Tony | 90 |
| Jim | 88 | Terry | 82 |
| Team total | 347 | Team total | 335 |
| Team average | 87 | Team average | 84 |

2. The difference between the two team averages is determined, and 80% of this difference is calculated. This is the number of points the team with the lower average receives for each of the 3 games shot at this meeting.

| | |
|---|---|
| Team A average | 87 |
| Team B average | 84 |
| Difference | 3 |
| | × .80 |
| Handicap | 2.40 = 2 points |

## ORGANIZING A LEAGUE

You might like to organize an archery league, either within a class or as an intramural or interscholastic activity. Archers often enjoy team camaraderie in a league setting, and sometimes a personal, below-average performance is offset by the good performance of a teammate. Hence, the pressure to score well is less acute in a team setting.

1. A master sheet for calculating team handicaps is provided below in case you would like to organize an archery league, either within a class or as an intramural or interscholastic activity. These calculations are done for every pair of teams participating. If there are an uneven number of teams, the team without an opponent must shoot to score their team average or better; they receive a victory for each game in which they shoot their average or better.

2. In most leagues a fourth "game" is awarded based on the total of the 3-game series. The team with the low average receives the number of points equal to their game handicap times 3. For the example above, Team B receives 6 points for the overall game. The necessity of trying to win this fourth game prevents the strategy of a team "giving away" a game, thus lowering their averages for the following week, if they see they are unlikely to win the current game.

3. Archers do not have scores upon which to base their averages at the first meeting of a league. In this case, each archer shoots 3 games at the first meeting; the average of the two highest games is used to calculate a handicap for the first meeting and for the second meeting. Thereafter, the average is based on the most recent 6 games.

# Handicap League—Weekly Match Total Scoresheet

Team _____

| Archer | Game avg |
|--------|----------|
|        |          |
|        |          |
|        |          |
|        |          |
| Team total |      |

High team total avg. _____

Low team total avg. _____

Difference _____

x .80

Team handicap _____

Team _____

| Archer | Game avg |
|--------|----------|
|        |          |
|        |          |
|        |          |
|        |          |
| Team total |      |

| Archer | Game 1 | Game 2 | Game 3 | Total |
|--------|--------|--------|--------|-------|
|        |        |        |        |       |
|        |        |        |        |       |
|        |        |        |        |       |
|        |        |        |        |       |
| Team game totals |  |      |        |       |
| Team handicap |   |        |        |       |
| Total + handicap |  |      |        |       |

| Archer | Game 1 | Game 2 | Game 3 | Total |
|--------|--------|--------|--------|-------|
|        |        |        |        |       |
|        |        |        |        |       |
|        |        |        |        |       |
|        |        |        |        |       |
| Team game totals |  |      |        |       |
| Team handicap |   |        |        |       |
| Total + handicap |  |      |        |       |

Highest total plus handicap (if any) wins. Ties count 1/2 win for each team.

Won _____ Lost _____

Won _____ Lost _____

4. Sometimes there are not enough archers to put an equal number on each team. Teams short an archer are given a ''blind.'' Each week the team average is calculated, and the team is assigned this score as if it were another archer. The handicap can then be calculated as if both teams had an equal number of archers. As each game is shot, an average is calculated for the team and is added to their total score to determine the winning team. Note that if the team as a whole shoots above average, the blind is above average, too; but if the team shoots below average, the blind is below average.

5. Archers who cannot attend in a given week can be given the opportunity to shoot a makeup score prior to the league meeting if time and facilities permit. An archer who simply does not attend causes his or her team to be penalized by their having to subtract 10% from his or her average in adding up their team total. The absentee is considered to have shot this score for the present meeting, but this score is not used in calculating the individual's running average.

# Selected Scoring Drill

## 1. Scoring by End
[Corresponds to Archery, Step 13, Drill 1]

### Group Management
- Reproduce the Scoring Worksheet that follows. Distribute 1 to each member of your class.
- You can assign your students to complete the worksheet in class or as a take-home assignment.

### Equipment
- 1 Scoring Worksheet per student
- Pencil

### Instructions to Class
- ''On your worksheet there are 8 targets with Xs scattered over them. These targets represent 8 scoring ends by an archer, with the Xs indicating the location of shot arrows.''
- ''Using the scoresheet at the bottom of the page, score this archer by following the scoring rules in Step 13 of Archery: Steps to Success.''

### Student Success Goal
- Score every end perfectly

## Scoring Worksheet

Name _____ Class _____ Date _____

*Directions*: Enter the value of each arrow for Ends 1 through 8 on the scorecard at the end of this worksheet. Total the hits and end score. Keep a running score.

End 1.

End 2. One arrow bounced out of the target, witnessed by an archer.

End 3. One arrow missed.

End 4.

End 5. One arrow passed through the target.

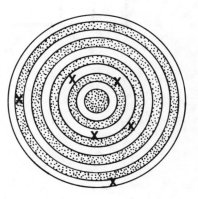

End 6.

End 7.

End 8. One arrow is embedded in the arrow in the 9-ring.

| End | Scorecard | | | | | Hits | End score | Running score |
|---|---|---|---|---|---|---|---|---|
| 1 | | | | | | | | |
| 2 | | | | | | | | |
| 3 | | | | | | | | |
| 4 | | | | | | | | |
| 5 | | | | | | | | |
| 6 | | | | | | | | |
| 7 | | | | | | | | |
| 8 | | | | | | | | |

Totals                    ——— ——— ———

## Answers to Scoring Worksheet

| End | Scorecard | | | | | | Hits | End score | Running score |
|---|---|---|---|---|---|---|---|---|---|
| 1 | 8 | 8 | 7 | 7 | 4 | 3 | 6 | 37 | 37 |
| 2 | 9 | 9 | 7 | 7 | 7 | 6 | 6 | 45 | 82 |
| 3 | 6 | 5 | 5 | 4 | 3 | 0 | 5 | 23 | 105 |
| 4 | 10 | 9 | 8 | 7 | 6 | 4 | 6 | 44 | 149 |
| 5 | 10 | 9 | 7 | 6 | 2 | 1 | 6 | 35 | 184 |
| 6 | 8 | 7 | 7 | 6 | 2 | 1 | 6 | 31 | 215 |
| 7 | 10 | 9 | 9 | 8 | 8 | 6 | 6 | 50 | 265 |
| 8 | 9 | 9 | 8 | 7 | 6 | 6 | 6 | 45 | 310 |

Totals  47  310  310

# Step 14  Tournament Shooting

Tournaments are traditionally the way target archers test their skills. Archers from many geographic regions, from various walks of life, with various types of equipment, of many ages and abilities, and of both sexes gather to see who can shoot the highest score. Tournaments are helpful in giving the target archer an event for which to prepare, a time to get equipment in order and to gather his or her energies.

In this way, a tournament can also be a good culminating experience for a class. Beginning archers can get a feel for the formalities of target archery (see Figure 14.1) and can be encouraged by this experience to pursue participation in archery tournaments outside the class setting. Where considerable interest in archery exists, perhaps fostered by your instruction program, an archery tournament can be a welcome intramural event or an interscholastic or intercollegiate competition. Tournaments can even be conducted with other institutions or clubs through the mail!

**Figure 14.1**  Tournament archers often dress in white.

## HOW TO ORGANIZE A TOURNAMENT

If an archery tournament is to be a positive experience for the participants, the tournament director must be highly organized. Archers appreciate a tournament that is run smoothly, fairly, and safely.

You will now review basic considerations in organizing a tournament. We will assume you have to direct a relatively extensive tournament, in the event this opportunity does arise; many of the resulting considerations can be set aside if you are merely running a tournament as the culminating experience of a beginning class.

## TOURNAMENT FORMAT

The first step in organizing a tournament is to decide which round will be shot. The size of the shooting range and the time available for shooting should be taken into consideration. As is apparent from the various tournament formats listed in Table 14.1 of *Archery: Steps to Success*, many choices are available. However, you, as tournament director, can also create the format used.

In either case, invitations to participate should state clearly what round or rounds will comprise the tournament. Particularly if the round is created or adapted from a standard round, the invitation should list the number of arrows to be shot—both in each end and for the entire tournament—the distances to be shot, and the target face to be used.

The number and types of shooting divisions must also be set. Archers can be placed in separate divisions by sex, by age, and by status (amateur, open, or professional). They can also be grouped by the type of equipment used: Common divisions are by type of bow (recurve versus compound), whether the equipment simulates that used for hunting, whether a bowsight is used, and whether the

fingers or a mechanical trigger hold the bowstring. It is best to use the equipment classifications specified by the various archery governing bodies. For example, a division only for recurve bows should follow equipment rules of the National Archery Association of the United States for all aspects of the shooting equipment. You should specify the shooting divisions you offer in the tournament on the invitation, as well as the equipment rules that you will use to separate shooters into divisions, and any limitations on the number of archers that you can accept.

## REGISTRATION

Registration can be simple and handled by one person or extensive and demand a committee of persons, depending upon the event you are organizing. Assuming the tournament is more extensive than a class event, you will probably need a registration form that requests a certain amount of information from the entrants. Depending upon the group you're inviting to participate, and the number and kinds of shooting divisions you will have, the following information may be desired:

- Name
- Address
- Age and sex
- Division entered
- Status (amateur, open, professional)
- Desired shooting time (if optional)

If a fee is required, this must be submitted to you with the registration form.

You should give some consideration to including a liability waiver similar to that suggested in Step 2. Also, in some tournaments target assignments are made in the order the registrations are received; if you use this method, you must number the registration forms as you receive them.

## SHOOTING RANGE

The shooting range must be in good order for a tournament. You must inspect the target mats to ensure that they will stop arrows. You should use only mats in good repair; then you can set the number of archers who can be accommodated in the tournament. Wind flags are helpful to archers in judging the wind; prepare them for the tournament if they are not used on a daily basis for classes (see Figure 14.2).

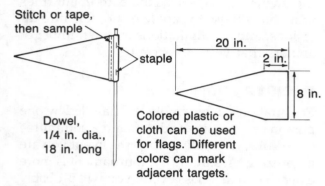

**Figure 14.2** Wind flags can be handmade.

You must clearly mark shooting lines for each shooting distance included in the tournament. Distance markers are sometimes provided, particularly in tournaments where archers change distances frequently. It is also desirable to mark the point on the shooting line directly in front of the target so that the archer can stand in the proper location.

A tournament is a good occasion on which to check the warning signs posted around the shooting range. This is particularly true because the tournament may be shot at a time the range is not normally used; if others regularly walk across the range when it is not in use, extra precautions for the tournament may be warranted. Extra signs could be posted, or the area could be roped off.

The number of target faces needed for the tournament must be determined ahead and ordered. It is customary to replace target faces when the area around a scoring line becomes so worn that it is difficult to score arrows landing in this area. Therefore, you should order extra target faces to allow for such replacements.

## FIELD CAPTAIN

The field captain runs the shooting line during the tournament, signaling for shooting to begin and for archers to go forward to score. The field captain also calls the score on borderline arrows when requested to by a target captain. If you, the instructor, do not serve as field captain, you should train others for this job before the tournament. They should be made aware of the scoring rules and of the proper procedures to follow in running the shooting line. In large tournaments several additional judges are designated to call borderline arrows.

## WEATHER

It is common to shoot archery tournaments in windy and rainy conditions, although rain delays can be granted by the tournament director if the conditions are severe. Shooting should always be stopped if lightning is in the area. The tournament director should be on hand to make the decision regarding a stoppage or should designate someone else to make this decision.

## SCORING

You must prepare scorecards before tournament day. As much as possible, design these cards specifically for the round shot (see Figure 14.3). When two scorecards will be kept on each archer, you must prepare twice the number of scorecards as shooters expected. It is desirable to have dual scoring in tournaments so that any questions about the accuracy or readability of a scorecard can be more easily settled. If archers preregister, it is helpful to place the archers' names and target assignments on the scorecards ahead of time. Distribution of scorecards, then, simultaneously informs archers of target assignments and provides them with scorecards.

When special instructions on how to fill out the scorecards are necessary, the field captain can give such instructions before shooting begins. Archers must be told whether you want them to submit both scorecards at the conclusion of shooting or whether one submission is sufficient and they may keep the other card for reference.

# Tournament Scorecard

Name _____     Sat. _____

Address _____     Sun. _____

City _____     Total _____

Age _____ Style _____ Sex _____ Event _____

Sat. Target # _____     Sun. Target # _____

**50 yards**

| E | 1 | 2 | 3 | 4 | 5 | 6 | End score | Run-ning |
|---|---|---|---|---|---|---|-----------|----------|
| 1 | | | | | | | | |
| 2 | | | | | | | | |
| 3 | | | | | | | | |
| 4 | | | | | | | | |

Total ⌐

**40 yards**

| | | | | | | | | |
|---|---|---|---|---|---|---|---|---|
| 5 | | | | | | | | |
| 6 | | | | | | | | |
| 7 | | | | | | | | |
| 8 | | | | | | | | |

Total ⌐

**30 yards**

| | | | | | | | | |
|---|---|---|---|---|---|---|---|---|
| 9 | | | | | | | | |
| 10 | | | | | | | | |
| 11 | | | | | | | | |
| 12 | | | | | | | | |

Total ⌐

**50 yards**

| E | 1 | 2 | 3 | 4 | 5 | 6 | End score | Run-ning |
|---|---|---|---|---|---|---|-----------|----------|
| 13 | | | | | | | | |
| 14 | | | | | | | | |
| 15 | | | | | | | | |
| 16 | | | | | | | | |

Total ⌐

**40 yards**

| | | | | | | | | |
|---|---|---|---|---|---|---|---|---|
| 17 | | | | | | | | |
| 18 | | | | | | | | |
| 19 | | | | | | | | |
| 20 | | | | | | | | |

Total ⌐

**30 yards**

| | | | | | | | | |
|---|---|---|---|---|---|---|---|---|
| 21 | | | | | | | | |
| 22 | | | | | | | | |
| 23 | | | | | | | | |
| 24 | | | | | | | | |

Total ⌐

Score check:

| | |
|----|---|
| 50 | |
| 40 | |
| 30 | |
| T | |

Scorer _____

Scorer _____

Shooter _____

(signatures)

Score check:

| | |
|----|---|
| 50 | |
| 40 | |
| 30 | |
| T | |

Scorer _____

Scorer _____

Shooter _____

(signatures)

**Figure 14.3** Sample tournament scorecard.

At the conclusion of shooting, post the scores (see Figure 14.4). For large tournaments, this may require a scoring committee. Prepare scoreboards ahead so that you can determine the final standings soon after the shooting.

## FREESTYLE LIM.
### MEN Code: AR03 ●

| | | SAT. | SUN. | Total | Place |
|---|---|---|---|---|---|
| John Black | Fenton | 632 | 655 | 1287 | S |
| Bill Jones | Fenton | 622 | 608 | 1230 | 4 |
| Dan Smith | Hallsville | 657 | 678* | 1335* | G |
| Keith Thomas | Hallsville | 563 | 548 | 1111 | 5 |
| Steve Cohn | Hazelwood | 612 | 628 | 1240 | B |
| | | | | | |
| | | | | | |
| *New Record | | | | | |

### WOMEN Code: AR04 ○

| | | | | | |
|---|---|---|---|---|---|
| Anne McMartin | St. Louis | 590 | 627 | 1217 | S |
| Joy Ford | Florissant | 610 | 616 | 1226 | G |
| Mary Thomas | Centerville | 600 | 615 | 1215 | B |
| Lydia Gray | St. Louis | 590 | 610 | 1200 | 4 |
| Jane Meyer | Florissant | 589 | 609 | 1198 | 5 |

**Figure 14.4** The standings board can be prepared ahead and scores filled in quickly after archers turn them in to tournament officials.

## AWARDS

You must also plan awards ahead of time. Determine the number of place awards, for example, three—gold, silver, and bronze. You must order or make this number of awards times the number of shooting divisions. You must make some provision for ties. If ties will stand, you will need extra awards. Obviously, if ties will be broken by a shoot-off or by counting the number of bull's-eyes shot, the number of hits, or so on, you can determine the exact number of awards ahead.

## PUBLICITY

Getting publicity for a tournament is often time consuming. However, you will obtain no publicity unless you make an effort to get publicity. Invitations to participate must give all the pertinent information clearly or at least tell a potential participant where to go for more information. Whenever possible, deliver notices to the media well ahead of time; this will increase the likelihood it is used.

It usually saves time to prepare standings sheets before the tournament. You can quickly enter the names and scores of winners at the conclusion of the tournament, and you can distribute the sheets to the media. It often helps to prepare a short explanation of archery tournaments and what archery scores mean for distribution with the standings.

## ADDITIONAL TYPES OF TOURNAMENTS

Archers are often attracted to tournaments that vary from the traditional and common ones. They can serve as changes of pace and unique challenges. If time permits, shooting several different types of tournaments can be an enjoyable culmination for an archery class. Several types of tournaments with distinct formats are explained below.

### The Knock-Down Round

Archery differs from many other individual sports in that archers are all competing against one another at the same time, rather than one-on-one. One type of archery tournament that features one-on-one competition is the knock-down round. Each archer is entered into a tournament bracket (see Figure 14.5) and shoots against another archer for a short number of ends. The winner by total score advances to the next round, and so on until a single winner is determined. A double-elimination format can also be used with an archer competing until he or she has two losses (see Figure 14.6). The entire round can be shot at once, but the scoring is conducted in opposed pairs.

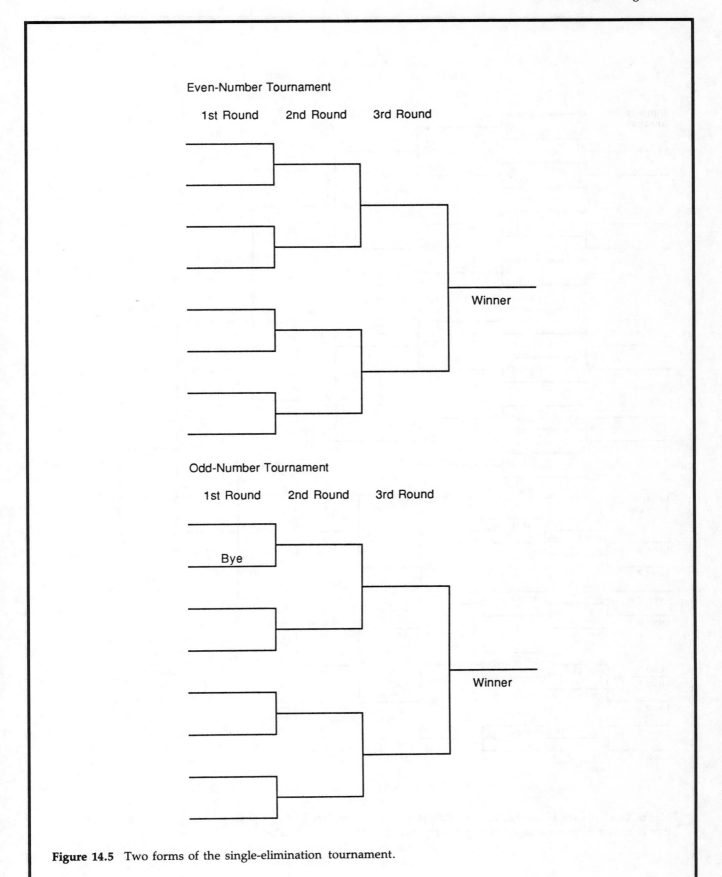

**Figure 14.5** Two forms of the single-elimination tournament.

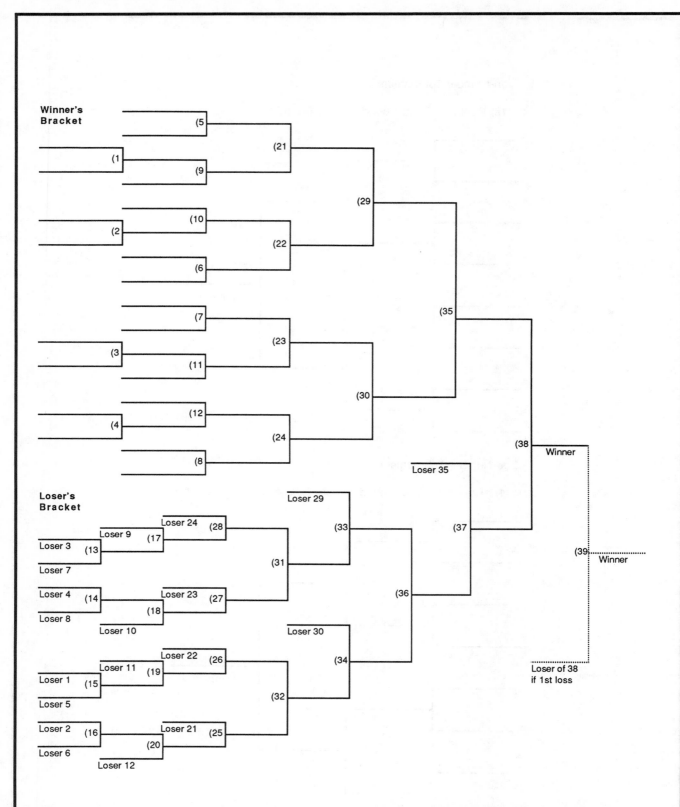

**Figure 14.6**  A sample bracket for a double-elimination tournament. Each pairing is assigned a number so that the loser of any pairing can be properly placed in the bottom bracket.

## The Clout Tournament

A clout tournament is an enjoyable change of pace for archers because it is so unique. The target is laid out on the ground and is 48 feet in diameter. Distances over 100 yards are shot in official tournaments, but any shooting distance from 65–100 yards is acceptable for class tournaments. Of course, you need a large area such as a football field.

The students with light-poundage bows must loft the arrows to hit the target. Have the student draw to the anchor as normal, then bend at the waist to raise the bow arm. The ideal elevation of the arm must be determined by trial and error. A special bowsight can be fashioned from a pencil attached to the lower limb with a rubber band (see Figure 14.7), with the pencil point serving as an aiming aperture.

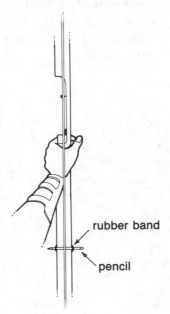

rubber band

pencil

**Figure 14.7** A bowsight for clout shooting can be made by attaching a pencil to the bottom limb with a rubber band. It can be moved up and down and right and left.

You should make a clout flag and scoring chain for the tournament. The clout flag is usually 30–36 inches square with a solid color disk—at most, 9.6 inches in diameter—in the center. The scoring chain can be chain, tape, or heavy rope, about 26 feet long. It should have a loop on either end. Starting from the center loop, it should be divided into 5 sections, each 4 feet 3 inches long, which correspond to the gold, red, blue, black, and white scoring rings on the traditional archery target face (see Figure 14.8). It is helpful to color the scoring chain or place colored tape on the chain.

All archers shoot their arrows at once, then go forward to score. The center loop of the scoring chain is placed over a stake under the clout flag. Five archers stand behind the chain, one per scoring section. One takes hold of the far loop, and all walk around in their respective circles, gathering the arrows whose tips are in the ground within their scoring ring.

After a full circle is swept, the arrows are grouped by fletch color or crest and laid across the appropriate section of scoring chain. The archers walk down the scoring chain with their scorecards, recording the values of their arrows. The archers then pick up their arrows and return for the next round. In a tournament, designated scorers can call out each archer's name in turn, so each archer can walk down the scoring chain, calling out the value of the arrows shot by him or her.

## The Field Round

A field round is another enjoyable tournament change of pace because most field rounds are laid out in wooded areas. Fourteen targets are scattered throughout the area, and archers walk and shoot from one to the next as in golf.

**Figure 14.8** A chain with the scoring rings marked off is used to score arrows that land in the ground near the target flag.

The distance shot at each target is unique, and archers may be required to shoot uphill, downhill, across a stream, and between trees (see Figure 14.9). A field range should have the appropriate distances marked; they are given in Table 14.1. Notice that target size also varies and a 4-arrow end is shot. A black-and-white target is used for field rounds. For a class tournament when light-poundage equipment is used, shooting can be from youth distances, which are shorter.

**Figure 14.9** Field archery is often shot on wooded, hilly terrain. Black-and-white target faces are used.

## Table 14.1  Field Round

| Distances shot (yd[a]) | Targets (cm) |
| --- | --- |
| The following distances are shot in four-arrow ends: | |
| 15, 20, 25, 30 | 35 |
| 40, 45, 50 | 50 |
| 55, 60, 65 | 65 |
| The following four-position shots consist of one arrow from each of four different positions: | |
| 35 | 50 |
| 45, 40, 35, 30 | 50 |
| 80, 70, 60, 50 | 65 |
| 35, 30, 25, 20 ft | 20 |

[a]All distances in yards, except for the four for the 20-cm target.

It may not be feasible to take your class to a field range, but you can hold a field round on your target range by having students change to a new distance on each end. Keep one target face of each size at each target butt; after scoring, students can put up the appropriate size of faces for the next end.

## The Animal Round

An animal round is particularly fun for archers interested in hunting. Animal rounds are usually shot on a field range, but at generally shorter distances than the field round. The targets are pictures of animals with two scoring rings marked (see Figure 14.10). An inner oval represents the kill area, and the outer ring follows the animal's profile and represents a wound area. Archers shoot a maximum of three arrows on each end. If they score with their first (20 for a kill and 16 for a wound), they stop. If they miss they shoot a second arrow, stopping if they score (14 for a kill and 10 for a wound). If they need a third arrow to score, they receive 8 for a kill and 4 for a wound. On some targets, archers move up to a closer distance on each arrow. The animal

**Figure 14.10**  Animal rounds are shot on field archery ranges, but paper animal targets are used.

targets come in three sizes, with smaller ones being used at closer distances.

An animal round can also be shot on a target range if it is not possible to visit a field range. The distances are usually odd ones: 32 yards instead of 30, 19 instead of 20, and so on. Students will have to interpolate from their even-yardage sight settings. You can also shorten the distances if the class is using light-poundage bows.

## Bowhunting Tournaments

Bowhunting tournaments are usually distinguished from others by the use of unknown shooting distances. Archers must be good at estimating their distance from the target, which is sometimes three-dimensional foam (see Figure 14.11), and using the appropriate sight setting. Only one shot at each target is allowed, and archers receive more points for an arrow landing in the kill zone than for hitting the target outside this zone. The shooting position is usually among the trees, rather than on a cleared path, if the range is in a wooded area. The archer must sometimes adapt stance, kneel, or squat to get a clear shot at the target.

You can adapt a bowhunting round for your target range. On each end, have archers shoot from different positions, such as sitting on a chair or kneeling (one knee or two), and have them shoot over or through a fallen tree branch moved to your range, a bale of hay, and so on. Paper animal targets can be used; these can be drawn by students rather than purchased.

## Archery Golf

Archery golf is another change-of-pace shoot and one that young archers particularly enjoy. You need a large space. You can set out a number of "holes," with a small group of archers walking from one to the next. The archer takes a shot toward the "hole." If the arrow does not hit the target, he or she takes a second, third, or fourth shot as needed from the place where the previous shot landed. Scoring is as in golf.

You can devise a number of types of targets. One of the easiest is to use traffic cones with blunt, rubber-tipped arrows (see Figure 14.12). You will need only 1 arrow per student, plus several spare arrows. You can make a small circle around each cone; any arrow striking the cone or landing in the circle is considered to be holed.

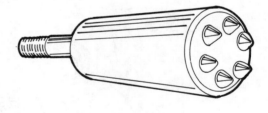

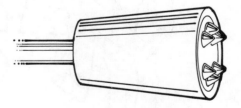

**Figure 14.12** Blunt-tipped arrows can be used for games like archery golf.

**Figure 14.11** Bowhunting rounds most often use 3D foam targets shaped like game.

# Step 15  The Mental Approach to Archery

In a class setting, the mental aspects of any sport are often overlooked. This may in part reflect the fact that the beginning student still needs to make much technical progress before the mental approach to performance can be a relatively significant contributor to success. However, it is obvious that the movements involved in shooting an arrow are relatively simple and that the preparation of the shot is the primary skill in archery. The mental approach, therefore, becomes relatively more important at an earlier stage in archery, compared to many other sports. The mental aspect of shooting is archery's unique challenge.

You can introduce your students to four aspects of mental preparation for performance. These are listed below with characteristics of performers at three skill levels—beginning, intermediate, and advanced. These descriptors will help you maximize the mental approaches of your students.

## Mental Approach Rating

| CRITERION | BEGINNING LEVEL | INTERMEDIATE LEVEL | ADVANCED LEVEL |
|---|---|---|---|
| Concentration | • Thinks about other events while shooting | • Thinks about details of form while aiming | • Concentrates on aiming once at full draw |
| Relaxation | • Is tense<br><br>• Has tension in hands | • Develops tension in hands and arms on important shots<br>• Cannot relax completely on cue | • Overcomes nervousness by concentrating<br>• Can relax hands, arms, neck on cue |
| Confidence | • Fails to set goals<br><br>• Believes bull's-eyes are hit almost by chance<br><br>• Outwardly expresses expectation of failure | • Sets goals too high or too low<br>• Worries after a missed shot that something has gone wrong with equipment or form<br>• Verbalizes failure when doesn't shoot well, and rationalizes failure as fault of equipment or shooting conditions | • Sets realistic and obtainable goals<br>• Believes every shot can be a bull's-eye<br><br><br>• Stops negative thoughts and verbalizes positive statements |

## Mental Approach Rating

| CRITERION | BEGINNING LEVEL | INTERMEDIATE LEVEL | ADVANCED LEVEL |
|---|---|---|---|
| Visualization | • Never visualizes | • Lets the image of a bad shot repeat itself | • Visualizes only successful shots<br><br>• Visualizes success after a bad shot |

# Error Detection and Correction for the Mental Approach

An archer often overlooks the mental approach to the game, agonizing instead over form or equipment. In fact, the flaw in the shooting may be in his or her mental approach. The mental approach is probably overlooked because the archer usually does not realize the approach is negative rather than positive, or does not realize the impact this can have on shooting.

You are instrumental in helping your students identify characteristics of the mental approach to their game. The corrections below assume that any of the errors listed are not truly the result of a physical form flaw or the equipment used.

**ERROR** 🚫

**CORRECTION**

1. Inconsistent shooting occurs.

1. Inconsistency can be traced to lapses in concentration. The archer who shoots inconsistently should practice the concentration drills and use a mental checklist on every shot.

2. Accuracy of shooting declines after one poor shot follows a period of good shooting.

2. The archer who experiences this may be holding the image of the bad shot and "replaying" it. Encourage your student to rehearse a good shot mentally after a poor actual one.

3. Student consistently fails to meet goals.

3. The goals set may be too high. Review the archer's goals with him or her and suggest changes.

4. Archer verbalizes negative statements about shooting.

4. Encourage the archer to recognize these statements with the help of those within earshot and to put them into a positive framework.

| ERROR | CORRECTION |
|---|---|
| 5. Archer talks excessively about form, analyzing it on every shot. | 5. Attention to the details of form may be detracting from concentration on aiming. Encourage the archer to forget about form once he or she anchors and to use the ''aim, aim, aim'' cue during aiming. |
| 6. Archer becomes tight and tense in critical shooting situations. | 6. It is natural to be nervous on important shots. Encourage the archer to accept this, to practice relaxing in order to relax on cue, and to attend to putting together the shot. |

# Selected Mental Approach Drills

## 1. *Verbal Cue Drill*
[Corresponds to *Archery*, Step 15, Concentration Drill 3]

### Group Management and Safety Tips
- Have students work in pairs and shoot from 20 yards.
- Distribute Arrow Pattern Analysis sheets to each student.

### Equipment
- Standard archery tackle for every student
- 1 target butt, an 80-cm target face, and bale pins for every four students
- Arrow Pattern Analysis sheets (see Step 8, Drill 3)

### Instructions to Class
- ''Work with a partner, alternately shooting and recording.''
- ''Shoot 2 six-arrow ends from 20 yards.''
- ''After each shot, report the location of your aiming aperture at release to your partner, giving the clock-face direction and scoring ring.''
- ''Partners, record the location the shooter reports by placing an **a** where your partner is aiming and put an **x** where the arrow lands.''

- ''Shooters, when you are ready to aim, say to yourself, 'Aim, aim, aim,' until release occurs.''

### Student Options
- ''Shoot from 30 yards.''
- ''Shoot from 40 yards.''

### Student Keys to Success
- Anchor
- Level your bow
- Align your string
- Say ''aim, aim, aim,'' until release

### Student Success Goal
- 12 repetitions aimed at the bull's-eye at release

### To Reduce Difficulty
- Let your student use a 122-cm target face.

### To Increase Difficulty
- Make your student shoot a longer distance.

# 2. Hand and Arm Relaxation Drill

[Corresponds to *Archery*, Step 16, Relaxation Drill 1]

## Group Management and Safety Tips

- Use this drill at the beginning of class (approximately 10 minutes).
- Conduct this activity in a quiet place where students can lie or sit comfortably.

## Equipment

- Tape or record of relaxing music

## Instructions to Class

- Give students the following cues in a quiet, soothing voice. Bracketed information tells you how long to have students hold tension, and when to repeat an exercise.

  *Sit or lie down and assume a comfortable position.*

  *Close your eyes.*

  *Bend your right hand back. Hold it tightly* [10 seconds]. *Relax* [repeat].

  *Bend your right hand forward. Hold it tightly* [10 seconds]. *Relax* [repeat].

  *Bend your left hand back. Hold it tightly* [10 seconds]. *Relax* [repeat].

  *Bend your left hand forward. Hold it tightly* [10 seconds]. Relax [repeat].

  *Bend your right hand back with half as much tension. Hold* [10 seconds]. *Relax* [repeat].

  *Bend your right hand forward with half as much tension. Hold* [10 seconds]. *Relax* [repeat].

  *Bend your left hand back with half as much tension. Hold* [10 seconds]. *Relax* [repeat].

  *Bend your left hand forward with half as much tension. Hold* [10 seconds]. *Relax* [repeat].

  *Bend your right hand back with just enough tension so that you feel the hold. Hold* [10 seconds]. *Relax* [repeat].

  *Bend your right hand forward with slight tension. Hold* [10 seconds]. *Relax* [repeat].

  *Bend your left hand back with slight tension. Hold* [10 seconds]. *Relax* [repeat].

  *Bend your left hand forward with slight tension. Hold* [10 seconds]. *Relax* [repeat].

  *Bend at your right elbow. Hold* [10 seconds]. *Relax* [repeat].

  *Bend at your left elbow. Hold* [10 seconds]. *Relax* [repeat].

  *Bend at your right elbow with half tension. Hold* [10 seconds]. *Relax* [repeat].

  *Bend at your left elbow with half tension. Hold* [10 seconds]. *Relax* [repeat].

  *Bend at your right elbow with slight tension. Hold* [10 seconds]. *Relax* [repeat].

  *Bend at your left elbow with slight tension. Hold* [10 seconds]. *Relax* [repeat].

  *Clench your right fist and tighten your whole right arm. Hold* [10 seconds]. *Relax* [repeat].

  *Clench your left fist and tighten your whole left arm. Hold* [10 seconds]. *Relax* [repeat].

## Student Option

- ''Tape this routine and do it by yourself sometime between classes.''

## Student Key to Success

- Feel the contrast between tensing and relaxing

## Student Success Goal

- Achieve a more relaxed state

## To Reduce Difficulty

- Drill is already in its easiest form.

## To Increase Difficulty

- Using the same procedure, add contrasts in the legs, trunk, and head region.

# 3. Mental Rehearsal

[Corresponds to *Archery*, Step 15, Confidence Drill 1]

## Group Management and Safety Tips

- Have students shoot from any distance that is a reasonable challenge for them.

## Equipment

- Standard archery tackle for every student
- 1 target butt, an 80-cm target face, and bale pins for every four students

## Instructions to Class

- "Practice as usual."
- "After any bad shot, mentally rehearse the feel of a good shot and see the arrow land in the bull's-eye. Your personal mental checklist can help you rehearse your shot."
- "Continue shooting."

## Student Option

- "Mentally rehearse a good shot after each and every shot."

## Student Keys to Success

- Repeat the cue "aim" as you are aiming
- Follow through

## Student Success Goal

- Mentally rehearse at least 12 shots

## To Reduce Difficulty

- Let student review a videotape of his or her shooting to facilitate mental rehearsal of a shot before this drill.

## To Increase Difficulty

- Make your student increase the shooting distance and mentally rehearse after every shot that is not a bull's-eye.

# 4. Thought-Stopping
[Corresponds to *Archery*, Step 15, Confidence Drill 3]

## Group Management and Safety Tips

- Assign four archers to a target.
- Give each archer a blank sheet of paper on a clipboard and a pencil.

## Equipment

- Standard archery tackle for every student
- 1 target butt, an 80-cm target face, and bale pins for every four students

## Instructions to Class

- "Shoot as normal, but any time you catch yourself thinking or verbalizing a negative statement about your performance, write out the negative statement."
- "Then write a positive counterpart."
- "At the end of class, we will discuss the statements you collected."

## Student Options

- "Write out any negative statements you catch yourself making about your archery ability between classes. Then write their positive counterparts."

- "Archers assigned together to a target can agree to help each other by catching any negative statements verbalized during class."

## Student Key to Success

- Expect to shoot well

## Student Success Goal

- 6 positive written statements about archery performance

## To Reduce Difficulty

- Drill is already in its easiest form.

## To Increase Difficulty

- Have your student repeat each positive statement to him- or herself 5 times after writing it.

# 5. Goal-Setting Drill
[Corresponds to *Archery*, Step 15, Confidence Drill 4].

## Group Management and Safety Tips

- Distribute a goal-setting sheet (see "Archery Goals") to each student at the beginning of class.

## Equipment

- Goal sheet and pencil for each student

## Instructions to Class

- "Before shooting today, consider your recent archery performance and write at least four goals."

- "You should write at least one goal for today's practice, one short-term goal, one intermediate-range goal, and one long-term goal."
- "Give a target date for achieving each goal."

## Student Option

- "Write out a goal for each archery class period, beginning with the current one."

**Student Key to Success**

- Establish goals that you can realistically meet

**Student Success Goal**

- Establish goals in all four time frames

**To Reduce Difficulty**

- Have your student write just immediate and short-term goals.

**To Increase Difficulty**

- Make your student write several goals for each time frame.

## Archery Goals

Name _____ Class _____ Date _____

| Time frame | | Goal | Target date | Date met | Instructor comment |
|---|---|---|---|---|---|
| Today | 1 | | Today | | |
| | 2 | | | | |
| | 3 | | | | |
| Short-term | 1 | | | | |
| | 2 | | | | |
| | 3 | | | | |
| Intermediate | 1 | | | | |
| | 2 | | | | |
| | 3 | | | | |
| Long-term | 1 | | | | |
| | 2 | | | | |
| | 3 | | | | |

## *Step 16*  Tuning Equipment

Tuning is a time-consuming process, but it teaches archers a great deal about how their equipment works. Also, tuning has, as its ultimate reward, the potential to increase scores greatly. Tuning involves setting up a bow specifically for an individual archer, so it may not be possible for your students to benefit from tuning because bows may be used in several classes or shared between classmates.

Even if it is not possible for students to tune their own bows, you can give them experience with tuning beyond their merely reading about it. For example, you may choose one student and one bow and spend a class period tuning that bow for the student, with all students participating in the decisions needed. This experience is enriched by using a bow with a cushion plunger. A pro shop owner may be willing to lend you a bow for this purpose. You can also have students go through some of the tuning steps, deciding how they would adjust their bows based upon their present performances. A worksheet is included at the end of this step. It can give students practice in making tuning decisions.

The following exercises are suggestions for giving your students some experience with aspects of bow tuning. They are described for recurve bows but can be adapted for compound bows by following Step 16 in *Archery: Steps to Success*. Students should use the tuning checklist in that same step as they proceed through this exercise.

***Tuning Exercise:*** In this exercise, students work through the preliminary adjustments in the tuning process, then tune their bows using the method you assign to them. The decision of which method to use depends on the availability of bare shafts and paper testing frames, and on the shooting space available.

- Each student has adapted and refined his or her form since last measuring the draw length. Remeasure the draw length, as done in Step 1, and have the student measure the actual draw weight at this draw length on a bow scale. If a scale is unavailable, your student can estimate draw weight by subtracting or adding 2 pounds per inch he or she is below or above, respectively, the standard printed on the bow.
- Each student should measure the string height on the bow to see that it is 6–8 inches for a straight-limb bow and approximately 8 inches for a recurve bow. If it is not, the archer can twist the bowstring to raise the string height or untwist it to lower the string height.
- Have your student add 3/4 inch to 2 inches to the draw length to determine the ideal arrow length. Using Table 16.1 in Step 16 of *Archery: Steps to Success*, the student should determine the ideal arrow size. If it is possible to fit your student with such arrows, he or she should continue the tuning process with these arrows. If not, the student can test the setup to decide what adjustments to make, but he or she may not be able to tune the bow perfectly to an incorrect arrow size.
- If the student has a cushion plunger on the bow, have him or her adjust the cushion plunger in or out to align the arrow as pictured in Figure 16.3 in Step 16 of *Archery: Steps to Success*.
- Your student should now use a bow square to check the position of the nock locator. It should be approximately 3/8 inch above the bottom of the bow square

as it barely rests on the arrow rest. If any nock locator varies greatly from this position, it should be adjusted. If it is close, though, it should be left in position for now because it will be adjusted in the tuning process.

- Assign the student a tuning method depending on whether you can change distances, have bare shafts matching students' arrows available, or have a paper testing frame available. You may have the student strip the fletching from one of the arrows to make a bare shaft, then have him or her refletch it in Step 17, "Maintaining Your Equipment." Paper testing frames are relatively easy to make from 2 × 2 inch lumber strips, using plywood for the legs (see Figure 16.1). The opening should be from 54–72 inches from the ground and approximately 36 inches wide. Tape newspaper over the opening.

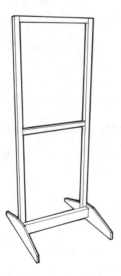

**Figure 16.1** Newspaper is taped to a wooden frame for paper tuning.

- Your student should proceed with the first step of the fine tuning method assigned—fletch clearance if paper testing, or porpoising if using the other methods. If paper testing, the student may proceed to the porpoising test. If not actually tuning the equipment, the student can decide whether any adjustments are necessary and, if so, what they are. Your student is then finished with this exercise. If tuning the equipment, the student should make the necessary adjustment and retest for porpoising, continuing until reaching the ideal result.

- The student who is actually tuning equipment should proceed to test for fishtailing, making adjustments until obtaining the ideal result. If the student did not previously test for fletch clearance, he or she should do it now.

***Alternate Tuning Exercise:*** If there are limitations on the equipment available to you, students may not be able to do the previous tuning exercise, but they can still get some limited experience with tuning. For example, you may not have a bow with a cushion plunger, but you can borrow one from a pro shop. In this case, you can do the following alternative tuning exercise.

- Your student should determine the ideal arrow shaft size and check the nock locator as described above.

- One student should proceed through the tuning steps, with the others participating in assessing the results and determining whether adjustments should be made and, if so, what the adjustments should be (use the Tuning Worksheet).

## Tuning Worksheet

Name _____ Class _____ Date _____

*Directions*: For each tuning method, the result of a porpoising or fishtailing test is given. Indicate what you would adjust and in what direction, as though you obtained this result while tuning a recurve bow with a cushion plunger. Assume that all of the appropriate preliminary steps have been taken.

I. Paper Testing: Pictures represent tears made by an arrow shooting through paper.

A.

B.

C.

Correction:

_____

_____

Correction:

_____

_____

Correction:

_____

_____

II. Bare Shaft Tuning: Symbols represent impact points of fletched and dots represent impact points of unfletched arrow shafts.

A.

B.

C.

Correction:

_____

_____

Correction:

_____

_____

Correction:

_____

_____

III. Variable Distance Tuning: Symbols represent impact points of arrows shot from 10–35 yards in 5-yard increments.

A.

B.

C.

Correction:

_____

_____

Correction:

_____

_____

Correction:

_____

_____

IV. Assume that after bare shaft tuning, you conduct a test for fletch clearance. You find that the top feather is making contact with the bow window. What adjustment would you make, and what would be the next step in tuning process?

_____

_____

_____

## Tuning Worksheet Answers

I. A. Move the nock locator down.
   B. Increase the spring tension of the cushion plunger or use a stiffer spring rest; decrease the poundage of a compound bow.
   C. No correction is necessary.

II. A. Move the nock locator down.
   B. No correction is necessary.
   C. Increase the spring tension of the cushion plunger, use a stiffer spring rest, or move the pressure point out; decrease the poundage of a compound bow.

III. A. Adjust the cushion plunger or pressure point inward.
   B. Increase the spring tension of the cushion plunger or use a stiffer spring rest.
   C. Adjust the cushion plunger or pressure point outward.

IV. After checking to assure that the bowstring is not catching on clothing, move the cushion plunger or pressure point out. The next step is to retune for fishtailing.

# Step 17  Maintaining Your Equipment

Archery equipment requires maintenance, especially when used by many different archers and by archers who are new at using the equipment. You have to maintain class equipment so that it can be used safely with maximum efficiency for many years.

At the same time, students should learn to maintain at least some equipment. If they purchase their own equipment at some time in the future, they would then be prepared to do some of their own maintenance. In learning maintenance, archers also learn more about their equipment and how variations in it affect shooting.

You may find that the most efficient way to maintain class equipment is to share some of these duties with your class. For example, if you must replace an arrow rest, demonstrate this to the class and have each student position the rest in the proper place before you permanently attach it to the bow. Also, bring bowstring wax to class and have students wax their own bowstrings.

You can have students learn maintenance as one of the final steps in the course. If maintenance is treated in one class period and you are limited in certain equipment such as arrow straighteners or fletching jigs, you may want to use a station organization or task method. Demonstrate the proper technique used at each station, then have your students rotate from station to station to complete the maintenance exercises. An alternative is to teach some of the maintenance procedures throughout the course as an individual student's equipment needs repair.

## REPLACING NOCKS

One frequent maintenance need is the replacing of nocks that have been cracked by other arrows striking the ends of arrows sitting in the target.

*Exercise 1:* Demonstrate to the students the proper way to replace a nock. Emphasize that just a small drop of fletching cement on the arrow taper and a small drop in the nock is sufficient. When the nock is placed on the arrow, turning it counterclockwise spreads the cement. Rotating it clockwise (screwing it onto the arrow) then seats it firmly.

After your demonstration, distribute one or more arrows to each student. Have replacement nocks available in containers marked with the sizes of the nocks. The student should remove the old nock with a dull knife, clean the surface, select the proper size of replacement nock (from Table 17.1 in *Archery: Steps to Success*), and cement the new nock in place. You should examine the finished product to be sure the nock is straight and properly aligned with the fletching.

## STRAIGHTENING ALUMINUM ARROWS

An arrow straightener is a relatively expensive accessory. If you are fortunate enough to have one for your program or can borrow one for a day, teach students to straighten their arrows.

*Exercise 2:* Demonstrate the proper way to straighten a bent arrow to the class. You will probably have just one student at a time straightening arrows, so other activities should be planned for the rest of the class. Have each student test the arrows he or she has been shooting in class for straightness on the arrow straightener and then straighten any that has a bend. You can later check the arrows to see that they have been properly straightened; you may find it faster simply to spin the arrows than to put them on an arrow straightener for this purpose.

## REPLACING A TARGET POINT

Target points do not often need replacing, but any archer who knows how to replace a point also knows how to initially install a point. This makes it possible for the archer to purchase bare arrow shafts, points, and fletching in order to build his or her own arrows. This skill can be a lifelong savings to the archer as well as an enjoyable addition to the sport.

*Exercise 3:* To have students learn to replace a target point, you need an alcohol burner, propane torch, or small gas flame. Caution students to be careful with the flame, then demonstrate how to remove, then replace, the point. Each student can use one of the arrows he or she has been shooting in class. Rather than need new points, your student can simply remove and replace the same point in an arrow shaft. You should examine the arrow when your student is finished to confirm that the tip is properly installed.

## FLETCHING ARROWS

Fletching eventually becomes worn and needs replacing. A new archer sometimes strips a feather or vane from a shaft by loading the arrow in the bow incorrectly, or by missing the target butt with a shot and having it fly against a hard object. Target archers usually prefer to refletch an entire arrow even if only one feather or vane needs replacing, but you may decide that replacing just one feather at a time is satisfactory for your class equipment.

*Exercise 4:* First demonstrate how to strip any of the old fletching and cement from the shaft with a dull knife and clean the shaft surface in the fletching area. This is important for getting a good bond between the fletching and arrow shaft. Show how to place an arrow into the fletching jig. Next, place a feather or vane into the clamp. It is helpful to mark clearly on the clamp itself exactly where along the clamp the feather or vane is to be placed. Stress that when applying fletching cement, only a small amount is needed. Also stress that no gaps

should be left in the cement line; the cement line should run the full length of the feather or vane. Finally, show your students how to place the clamp into the jig with the base of the fletching against the arrow shaft.

Unless you use fast-drying cement, you should allow at least 15 minutes for the fletching cement to dry. The number of arrows that can be fletched during a class period at this rate is limited. You may want to place your students into small groups for this fletching exercise.

It is best to purchase all right-hand wing or all left-hand wing feathers, depending upon which type was originally placed on the arrows, when providing students with the raw materials for refletching arrows. If you can keep the same type on all the arrows used in your program, you should be able to avoid having arrows with some of each type of fletching.

Consistency in feather or vane size and shape is important as well. Vanes and feathers come in different lengths, with larger sizes typically used on longer and heavier arrows. It is easiest to instruct students to use the same length of replacement fletching as the original. If you are fletching a set of arrows for the first time, fletching of about 3 inches length is probably adequate for most of your class arrows. Also, it is best to keep the color pattern of one index feather distinct in color from the other two, particularly when beginners use the arrows being fletched.

## WAXING A BOWSTRING

Waxing a bowstring is a simple maintenance procedure, but it extends the life of the bowstring. Periodically test the bowstring by running your fingers up and down the string to see whether it feels waxy. If not, it is time to rewax the string.

*Exercise 5:* Students have a tendency to put too much wax onto their strings the first time they wax. Demonstrate rubbing the wax onto the bowstring once or twice, on both the upper and lower sections (see Figure 17.1). The serving need not be waxed. Run your thumb and forefinger up and down the length of the string to work in the wax. Have each student wax the string on his or her own bow.

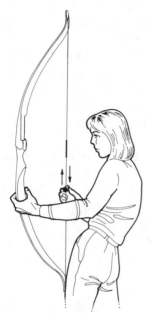

**Figure 17.1** Bowstrings are waxed by rubbing the wax on the string, then working it into the strands by rubbing the string with the fingers. The center and end servings need not be waxed.

## REPLACING A BOWSTRING

Bowstrings eventually become worn and frayed and should be replaced. New bowstrings should be purchased in a length about 4–4 1/2 inches shorter than the bow length, which is printed on the bow itself. After the bowstring is placed on the bow, the string height should be checked. A straight-limb bow should have a string height of 6–8 inches, and a recurve bow should have a height around 8 inches, unless the manufacturer specifies otherwise.

The number of strands in the bowstring should be 8 for bows under 25 pounds, and 10 for bows between 25 and 35 pounds. Thicker bowstrings than recommended can be used, but often the small nocks on the small shafts used by archers requiring lighter poundage fit

too tightly on a thicker string. This is detrimental to good arrow flight, so it is better not to vary too far from the recommended string thickness. Remember that a new nock locator has to be installed on the new bowstring.

## WAXING A BOW

The life of your class bows can be extended if they are periodically waxed with a good furniture wax. It is probably sufficient to have each student wax a bow once during the course.

## REPLACING AN ARROW REST

Most arrow rests eventually need to be replaced. A beginner can be particularly hard on an arrow rest, particularly if he or she pinches the arrow nock when drawing, thus pushing the arrow down as it sits on the rest.

The installation of a replacement rest varies slightly, depending on whether the bow is equipped with a cushion plunger. If it is, place an arrow onto the bowstring and adjust the placement of the arrow rest so that the middle of the arrow shaft contacts the middle of the plunger button. The rest should be level, not slanted up or downward, and positioned so that the arrow sits on the rest close to the cushion plunger, not behind or ahead of it. You can mark the position of the rest on the bow after determining the proper location; then remove the backing from the adhesive for final installation.

Class equipment is not likely to have cushion plungers, and replacement rests have both pressure points and arrow rests. The following exercise assumes this is the type of rest to be installed.

*Exercise 6:* You typically have only one or two arrow rests that need replacement at one time. You can give the entire class experience in replacing one, however, by having each student determine the proper location for a rest without permanently installing it. Demonstrate the proper location for the pressure point and arrow rest assembly. Stress that the center of the pressure point should be directly above the pivot point of the bow handle and that the height of the assembly should be set so that the bottom of the arrow is 5/8 inch above the bow shelf (see Figure 17.2). Check the location each student decides upon.

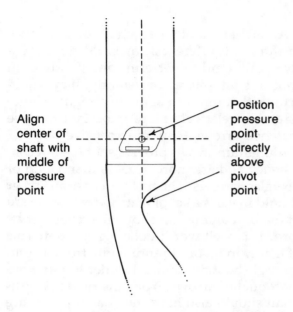

Align center of shaft with middle of pressure point

Position pressure point directly above pivot point

**Figure 17.2** Replacement arrow rests should be accurately positioned.

## MAINTAINING TARGET BUTTS AND FACES

As instructor, you have the additional responsibility of maintaining the target butts and the target faces. You can extend the life of a target face by placing tape on the back of the target face in places that become worn. Tape sold for sealing boxes works well for this purpose. Patches for the bull's-eye area of target faces are also sold commercially. These may be an economical way of lengthening the life of a target face, but be sure that you match the scoring lines of the patch with those on the target face.

You should moisten woven grass target mats occasionally. This causes the fibers to swell, stopping arrows better and resulting in less breakage of the grass fibers than would occur if they were dry. The manufacturer usually provides directions for the care of such mats; you should carefully follow these to prolong the lives of the mats. Also, store mats so that air can circulate between them; that is, do not stack them one directly on top of the other, because there is a chance of spontaneous combustion of the mats if you do this.

# Step 18 Upgrading Equipment

Improving equipment can improve scoring accuracy at any time, but this is a step best taken once your student archers have solidified their shooting forms, reached levels near their potential bests with the equipment they have, and have decided the types of archery (target shooting, bowhunting, etc.) they enjoy the most. Students who become interested enough to purchase their own equipment may well ask you how they should best spend their money. In addition, you may be interested in upgrading your class equipment. In this step, a priority list and a rationale for upgrading equipment are suggested.

## PRIORITY LIST
## FOR UPGRADING EQUIPMENT

Experienced archers and pro shop owners have their own opinions as to what kinds of equipment are the most important. Often, an archer's individual interests and shooting level can make a difference as to what equipment additions are the most important. For example, the archer who consistently creeps forward before release or releases before aiming and settling probably needs a clicker-type draw check before any of the equipment listed below. The priority list below is only a place to start, a list for the "average" archer from which individual considerations can be made.

*1. Arrows:* Consistency in both form and equipment is important to scoring accuracy. It is particularly important for arrows to be consistent in the manner they bend around the bow handle upon release. When an archer aims two shots identically and executes the shots as identically as humanly possible, the two arrows should perform identically. The arrows should clear the bow in the same way, with the same amount of bend.

An archer shoots the same bow from shot to shot, but different arrows. Even inexpensive bows tend to perform consistently from shot to shot—more consistently than would arrows that differ in spine or weight. Therefore, it is relatively more important to have matched arrows than an expensive bow.

Aluminum arrows provide shot-to-shot consistency and are more durable than wood or fiberglass arrows. The first purchase an archer should make is a set of matched arrows made of the best aluminum alloy the archer can afford. It is well worth delaying the purchase of a bow in favor of renting one from a commercial shooting range, in order to purchase high-quality arrows. Your instructional program should also have the goal of providing students with matched aluminum arrows.

*2. Upgrading the Bow:* Each archer must decide, based on the type of archery he or she enjoys the most and on what types of competition he or she might enter, if any, whether he or she wants a recurve or compound bow. Both come in a wide variety of models and price ranges.

In purchasing a recurve bow, the first consideration is to purchase a center-shot bow; the second consideration is to purchase a takedown bow. An archer who anticipates shooting competitively will eventually add at least one stabilizer and an extension sight; the bow should be tapped for these accessories. Both the handle riser and the limbs of take-down bows are available in a variety of materials. It is probably best for the novice archer to inquire about the advantages and disadvantages of each when visiting with a salesperson and to match archery interests to the advantages of certain materials. It is also valuable to ask experienced archers their opinions of various bows.

Compound bows with the pulleys mounted between a split in the bow limbs are generally more expensive than those with the pulleys mounted on a bracket attached to the limbs (see Figure 18.1). Archers should consider purchasing bows with split limbs if they anticipate shooting competitively. Compound bows are available with round, eccentric pulleys or with cams and, like the modern recurve bow, in a variety of materials. Asking both salespeople and experienced archers about advantages and disadvantages is a good strategy in purchasing the compound bow, as well as the recurve bow.

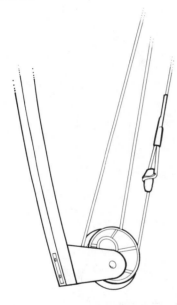

**Figure 18.1** Inexpensive compound bows sometimes have an eccentric pulley mounted on a bracket attached to the limb.

The novice archer need not feel that upgrading his or her bow from inexpensive or class equipment means purchasing the most expensive bow. Fortunately, moderately priced equipment today is consistent, reliable, and durable if properly maintained. Equipment in the moderate price range can be more than adequate while the archer continues to perfect his or her form and decides at what level to shoot. Bows themselves are constantly being perfected in both design and material. The latest advances that are incorporated into top-of-the-line models may not be needed by the archer until ready to shoot in top-flight competition.

***3. Stabilizers:*** An archer usually finds that arrow groups tighten when he or she adds a stabilizer to the bow. This is the result of the stabilizer minimizing the torque of the bow in the archer's hand upon arrow release (see Figure 18.2). Therefore, a stabilizer should be one of the first bow accessories purchased. The archer typically begins with a single stabilizer extended from the back of the bow, but the length and weight should be determined by what feels best to the individual archer.

***4. Arrow Rest Assemblies:*** Not only must equipment be of good quality, it must be matched to the archer. In other words, equipment should be tuned to the archer. A much larger range of tuning adjustments is available to the archer with an arrow rest assembly that includes either a cushion plunger (for recurve or compound bows) or a spring rest (usually for compound bows). Many styles are available. It is valuable for the archer to inquire of both salespeople and experienced archers as to the advantages and disadvantages of each style, and as to which models perform so well that it is worth spending a few more dollars on them.

***5. Extension Sights:*** The first consideration in purchasing an improved sight is to have it extended away from the bow. This, of course, provides finer sighting. Target sights made as extension sights usually allow the archer to select from a variety of aiming apertures, an additional advantage.

## IDEAS FOR CLASSES ON UPGRADING EQUIPMENT

You can consider planning a class on upgrading equipment at the end of your instructional program. You can adapt this class to the interests of your students. If your students are interested in target archery, you can contact

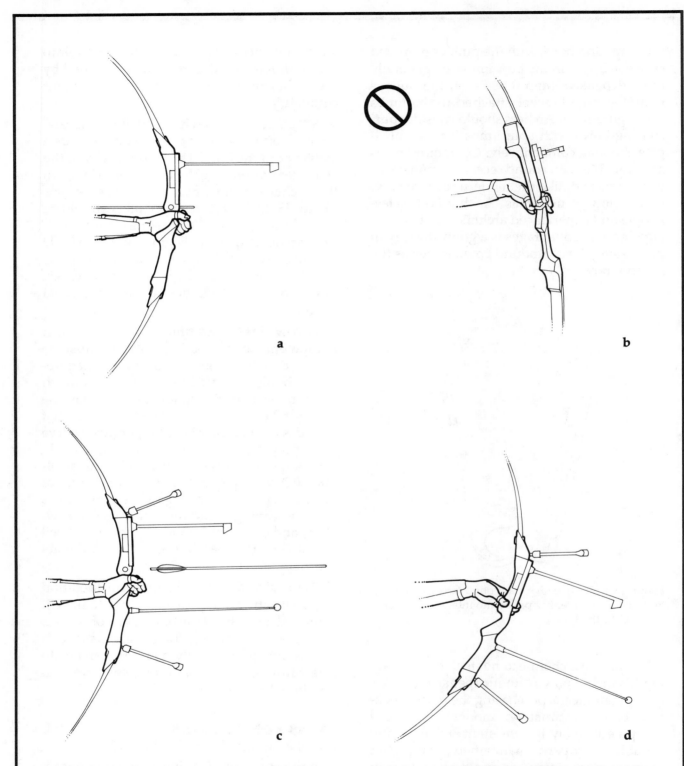

**Figure 18.2**   Without a stabilizer (a, b), the bow turns in the hand upon release. With a stabilizer (c, d), it falls forward, staying in a straight line to the target.

a local target club to see whether a member is available to visit your class and demonstrate his or her equipment. If your students are interested in bowhunting or bowfishing, contact a local bowhunting club and invite a member to class. This person can not only demonstrate equipment, but he or she can talk about how to dress for hunting and how to get started. A local pro shop owner may also be willing to visit your class, bringing examples of many accessories. Such a person can also answer students' questions about the current costs of archery equipment.

Seeing equipment and how it is used always means more to students than written descriptions or pictures of equipment. They may also find it interesting to speak with someone who enjoys archery as a hobby or profession. Students who have developed some interest in archery as a result of your instructional program can be even more motivated to pursue their interests after the course by a visit from someone else who is obviously enthused about archery.

# Evaluation Ideas

The many special features in the participant's book, *Archery: Steps to Success*, build in an ongoing, daily evaluation system. The "Keys to Success" list those biomechanical aspects of performance that describe correct body positioning or technique. The "Keys to Success Checklists" allow qualitative assessments by a trained peer, teacher, or coach of students' technique. The "Student Keys to Success" in this instructor's book combine and integrate the numerous, discrete body positions to help the learner sequence movements in a fluid manner, which the learner cannot be expected to do early in the learning process. The "Success Goals" in both books are quantitative assessments of your students' performance.

## COMBINING QUANTITATIVE AND QUALITATIVE EVALUATION

It is important to combine both quantitative and qualitative evaluations in order to satisfy the varying needs and abilities of typical beginning students. By your combining qualitative and quantitative evaluations, students who are less skilled, not very strong, or not very experienced will soon learn that they can earn "A's" in technique (by following the Keys to Success). This motivates them to practice, and their performance scores tend to improve, also. By using only quantitative evaluations, on the other hand, you would be creating desperate learners and rewarding only the highly skilled, the physically fit, and the most experienced students taking your beginning course.

### Influence of Equipment Fit

As instructor, you must also keep in mind that quantitative evaluation by the score an archer obtains reflects in part the "goodness" of equipment fit. The better fit a student is by

assignment of a particular bow and set of arrows, the higher the potential to score well. Two archers with identical technique can score quite differently if one is fit poorly and the other well. If you are able to fit all of your students equally well, quantitative evaluations by score are fair. However, if you do not have ample equipment and some students are fit well (even by chance) while others are not, such evaluations are very unfair. Your equipment situation, therefore, may dictate how much emphasis you place on target scores, or absolute scores, as a means of evaluation.

### Directional Error

If it is not appropriate to emphasize absolute scores (i.e., setting a criterion score to reach for a certain grade or comparison) in your situation, you might instead emphasize quantitative evaluation by directional errors. A student can center arrow groups around the bull's-eye even without the best fit of equipment. A better fit would simply tighten the archer's group, that is, reduce the dispersion of arrows around the bull's-eye, resulting in more arrows landing in higher scoring rings. The presence of a directional error indicates a flaw in execution of the shot, and the number of directional errors can be used as a means to evaluate execution. You can use the Arrow Analysis Chart to quantitatively assess your students (see Step 8, Drill 3). Note that the Technique Analysis Chart (see Step 8, Drills 1 and 2) corresponds to the qualitative (technique) objectives and their accompanying criteria.

## AN INDIVIDUAL PROGRAM

A Sample Individual Program is provided (see Appendix E.1) to illustrate evaluation by both qualitative and quantitative (by score) assessments. A blank program sheet is also located in Appendix E.2 for you to fill in your own qualitative and quantitative assessments, ratios, symbols, or percentages. To best adapt this evaluation system for your specific situation, you need to decide four things: (a) the total number of skills and concepts you want to assess; (b) the specific criteria that you want to observe qualitatively; (c) how much weight you want to place on any one skill, concept, or aspect of technique, based on the amount of practice time available, the inherent difficulty level, and—in the case of scoring assessment—equipment fit; and (d) the type of grading system that you prefer or must use, for example, letter grades (D, C, B, A), unsatisfactory/satisfactory, numbers (1, 2, 3, 4), symbols (bronze, silver, gold), or percentages (25, 50, 75, 100).

Whether or not you emphasize scoring in your evaluation program, you may want to have students keep score on a regular basis. Examination of scoresheets after class can identify the students who need your special attention during the next class. Frequent experience with scoring is helpful in teaching students proper scoring methods. Some students also tend to perform better if their scores are recorded, even if it is not a score that contributes to their final evaluation.

Masters are provided here for two types of daily scorecards. One contains four copies of Individual Scorecards that can be reproduced, perhaps on card stock, and cut apart. Note that there is space to record a daily average score per arrow. This average can be plotted on a graph to indicate the progress the archer makes over days of practice. The other master is of a single, Target Scoresheet that can be used for as many as four archers assigned to one target butt. Note that there is space for recording the distance each end is shot, in case several distances are shot during one class period.

It is recommended that you hand out your evaluation program sheets at your first class meeting. This encourages students to practice and improve, especially if they can assess each other on the quantitative evaluations up to a B level, but they must demonstrate for you (and get your initials) to receive an A level. This avoids a one-chance pressure situation for the students as they get used to performing in front of others, including you. Note that in the Sample Individual Program, performance criteria are included that are appropriate only at certain times during the course. For example, two criteria are included for shooting without a bowsight; once the class reaches Step 7, though, shooting for the remainder of the course is done with a sight. If you hand out your evaluation program sheets at your first class meeting, students can prepare for their early assessments.

You may want to designate a few days near the end of your unit as the final testing days in which students can still improve their scores to qualify for the A or top evaluation level. This will prevent your students from trying to increase their performance and technique scores beyond the deadline you set.

## ADAPTING INDIVIDUAL PROGRAMS

If you are working with very large classes spanning three or more grade levels, select fewer objectives. Allow peers to assess qualitative objectives up to a certain level of performance, for example, a B grade. Peers can also certify scores shot or arrow groups plotted while you are supervising, that is, serving as field captain.

If it is necessary to reduce the number of objectives that students are challenged to meet, we suggest that you be sure to retain the eight technique objectives addressing components of the basic archery shot. Then you can include one or two quantitative or performance objectives, either attaining a certain score, analyzing arrow groupings, or one of each.

You are likely to have several students who are either very far behind or very advanced compared to the majority of students. For example, you might have several students who have previous experience in archery and own

**Individual Scorecard**

Name                         Class

| Date | Yards | 1 | 2 | 3 | 4 | 5 | 6 | Total | Daily avg. |
|------|-------|---|---|---|---|---|---|-------|------------|
|  |  |  |  |  |  |  |  |  |  |
|  |  |  |  |  |  |  |  |  |  |
|  |  |  |  |  |  |  |  |  |  |
|  |  |  |  |  |  |  |  |  |  |
|  |  |  |  |  |  |  |  |  |  |
|  |  |  |  |  |  |  |  |  |  |
|  |  |  |  |  |  |  |  |  |  |
|  |  |  |  |  |  |  |  |  |  |
|  |  |  |  |  |  |  |  |  |  |
|  |  |  |  |  |  |  |  |  |  |
|  |  |  |  |  |  |  |  |  |  |
|  |  |  |  |  |  |  |  |  |  |

**Individual Scorecard**

Name                         Class

| Date | Yards | 1 | 2 | 3 | 4 | 5 | 6 | Total | Daily avg. |
|------|-------|---|---|---|---|---|---|-------|------------|
|  |  |  |  |  |  |  |  |  |  |
|  |  |  |  |  |  |  |  |  |  |
|  |  |  |  |  |  |  |  |  |  |
|  |  |  |  |  |  |  |  |  |  |
|  |  |  |  |  |  |  |  |  |  |
|  |  |  |  |  |  |  |  |  |  |
|  |  |  |  |  |  |  |  |  |  |
|  |  |  |  |  |  |  |  |  |  |
|  |  |  |  |  |  |  |  |  |  |
|  |  |  |  |  |  |  |  |  |  |
|  |  |  |  |  |  |  |  |  |  |
|  |  |  |  |  |  |  |  |  |  |

**Individual Scorecard**

Name                         Class

| Date | Yards | 1 | 2 | 3 | 4 | 5 | 6 | Total | Daily avg. |
|------|-------|---|---|---|---|---|---|-------|------------|
|  |  |  |  |  |  |  |  |  |  |
|  |  |  |  |  |  |  |  |  |  |
|  |  |  |  |  |  |  |  |  |  |
|  |  |  |  |  |  |  |  |  |  |
|  |  |  |  |  |  |  |  |  |  |
|  |  |  |  |  |  |  |  |  |  |
|  |  |  |  |  |  |  |  |  |  |
|  |  |  |  |  |  |  |  |  |  |
|  |  |  |  |  |  |  |  |  |  |
|  |  |  |  |  |  |  |  |  |  |
|  |  |  |  |  |  |  |  |  |  |
|  |  |  |  |  |  |  |  |  |  |

**Individual Scorecard**

Name                         Class

| Date | Yards | 1 | 2 | 3 | 4 | 5 | 6 | Total | Daily avg. |
|------|-------|---|---|---|---|---|---|-------|------------|
|  |  |  |  |  |  |  |  |  |  |
|  |  |  |  |  |  |  |  |  |  |
|  |  |  |  |  |  |  |  |  |  |
|  |  |  |  |  |  |  |  |  |  |
|  |  |  |  |  |  |  |  |  |  |
|  |  |  |  |  |  |  |  |  |  |
|  |  |  |  |  |  |  |  |  |  |
|  |  |  |  |  |  |  |  |  |  |
|  |  |  |  |  |  |  |  |  |  |
|  |  |  |  |  |  |  |  |  |  |
|  |  |  |  |  |  |  |  |  |  |
|  |  |  |  |  |  |  |  |  |  |

## Target Scoresheet

Class

Date

Target Number

Name

| Name | | | | | | | |
|------|---|---|---|---|---|---|---|
| Yds. | 1 | 2 | 3 | 4 | 5 | 6 | Total |

| Name | | | | | | | |
|------|---|---|---|---|---|---|---|
| Yds. | 1 | 2 | 3 | 4 | 5 | 6 | Total |

| Name | | | | | | | |
|------|---|---|---|---|---|---|---|
| Yds. | 1 | 2 | 3 | 4 | 5 | 6 | Total |

| Name | | | | | | | |
|------|---|---|---|---|---|---|---|
| Yds. | 1 | 2 | 3 | 4 | 5 | 6 | Total |

their own equipment. It is still appropriate for these students to meet the eight technique objectives addressing components of the basic shot. However, you can challenge these students to meet more extensive objectives for error analysis or the mental approach to shooting. You can also challenge them to meet more stringent performance objectives in any one of a number of ways: You can raise their scoring goals or have them shoot rounds at longer distances or on smaller target faces.

Students who are very small or weak compared to the average can find it difficult to match the performance objectives set for the class. This is particularly true if the equipment available is sized for larger and stronger individuals. You might be able to obtain more appropriate equipment through a pro shop or a local archery club where families may have equipment outgrown by young archers. It is particularly helpful for a small archer to have relatively short bows, the limbs providing more cast at the archer's draw length than would a longer bow. You can adjust performance objectives by shortening shooting distances or using larger target faces.

# Test Bank

You might have included a written examination in planning your individual program. If so, the sample questions below will be helpful. You can use as many as you wish, depending on the number of steps covered. You can also use these questions as models for generating additional questions in the areas you would like to emphasize in greater depth. You may wish to present some or all of the following questions in a test booklet that is reusable. In this case, design an answer sheet that students could circle or mark over.

## WRITTEN EXAMINATION QUESTIONS

*True/False Directions*: Please write "True" or "False" in the space at the left side of the question number.

_____ 1. An arrow hitting the wrong target counts as much as if it had hit the correct target.

_____ 2. If an archer shoots 7 arrows instead of 6, the specified number per end, the lowest arrow is not counted.

_____ 3. An arrow that lands on a line between two scoring rings on the target receives the higher value.

_____ 4. An arrow hitting the blue ring and rebounding, witnessed by another archer, is scored as 7 points.

_____ 5. As distance increases, the sight aperture moves down the sight bar.

_____ 6. *Cast* means the accuracy with which a bow propels an arrow.

_____ 7. The correct length of an arrow for an individual archer is determined by the weight of the bow the archer is using.

_____ 8. The anchor point should be moved forward and back according to distance from the target.

_____ 9. It is good practice in testing a bow to draw it without an arrow, then let go.

_____ 10. Archers should pull arrows from the target by grasping the shaft close to the target face and twisting the arrow out of the target.

_____ 11. The longer an archer's draw length, the higher the poundage shot with a recurve bow.

_____ 12. Anchoring with the jaw open is likely to cause a high arrow.

_____ 13. A possible cause of the arrow falling off the arrow rest during draw is the archer not keeping the back of the draw hand straight and relaxed.

_____ 14. If an archer shoots a group of arrows to the left of the bull's-eye, he or she should move the sight aperture to the left.

_____ 15. When archers are on the shooting line and the whistle is blown once, they may nock their arrows.

_____ 16. The bow should be held with all the fingers of the bow hand rigidly extended.

_____ 17. When the bow arm is extended in the shooting position, the back of the bow is toward the archer.

_____ 18. An arrow that passes through the target face and butt does not count.

_____ 19. Arrows made from aluminum are more consistent than those made from wood.

_____ 20. Bows with recurve-shaped limbs first became available to archers in the twentieth century.

_____ 21. Archery first became an Olympic event in 1972.

_____ 22. Women have been competing in archery contests for at least 300 years.

_____ 23. A compound bow has a pulley or cam incorporated into its construction.

_____ 24. The longer an archer's draw length, the longer the ideal bow length.

_____ 25. Thought-stopping is the technique wherein archers concentrate only on aiming after they draw.

_____ 26. The best goals an archer can set are intermediate goals that are easy to attain.

_____ 27. The last step in bow tuning is adjustment of the nock locator.

_____ 28. Archers often fletch their arrows with feathers for indoor shooting and vanes for outdoor shooting.

_____ 29. A kisser button aids in achieving a consistent anchor position.

_____ 30. The bow sling prevents an archer from gripping the bow too low on the handle.

_____ 31. Canting the bow to the right is likely to cause arrows to land left on the target (right-hander).

_____ 32. Peeking to watch the arrow in flight is likely to cause arrows to land right on the target (right-hander).

_____ 33. Allowing the wrist to break right (hyperextend) on release is likely to cause arrows to land left on the target (right-hander).

_____ 34. Gripping the bow too tightly is likely to cause arrows to land high on the target (right-hander).

_____ 35. Dropping the bow arm at release is likely to have no effect on the arrow.

_Multiple Choice Directions_: Please write in the correct letter in the space at the left side of the question number.

_____ 1. Which fingers does a right-handed archer place on the bowstring?
   a. All of the fingers
   b. The index finger and thumb
   c. The middle three fingers
   d. The middle three fingers and the thumb

_____ 2. With the bow arm extended, in position for the draw, how should the arrow be positioned for a right-handed archer?
   a. Left of the bow, index feather to the right
   b. Right of the bow, index feather to the left
   c. Right of the bow, index feather to the right
   d. Left of the bow, index feather to the left

_____ 3. How are the draw fingers placed on the bowstring?
   a. In the first joints
   b. In the second joints
   c. Onto the fingertip pads
   d. Between the first and second joints

_____ 4. What should an archer feel when drawing the bow correctly?
   a. The bow shoulder roll up and forward
   b. The shoulder blades moving toward each other
   c. The shoulder blades moving apart
   d. Tension in the upper arm

_____ 5. How can an archer prevent the bowstring from hitting the bow arm or wrist?
   a. By raising the left shoulder
   b. By grasping the bow handle from the side
   c. By rotating the bow elbow away from the path of the string
   d. By using a lighter bow

_____ 6. In what position should the draw arm be at full draw?
   a. Positioned with the elbow below shoulder level
   b. Positioned with the draw arm at shoulder level
   c. Positioned with the elbow pointing down the shooting line
   d. Positioned with the elbow tucked close to the chest

_____ 7. Which of the following is good aiming technique?
   a. Holding the aperture steady in the bull's-eye
   b. Moving the bow so the aperture passes through the bull's-eye, and releasing
   c. Moving the bow so the aperture moves slowly into the bull's-eye, and releasing
   d. Releasing as soon as the bull's-eye is seen

_____ 8. A bow should always be unbraced by removing the loop(s) from which of the following?
   a. The top limb
   b. The bottom limb
   c. Either limb
   d. Both limbs

_____ 9. Which statement is true about the shooting position?
   a. Toe the shooting line with your front foot
   b. Heel the shooting line with the back foot
   c. Straddle the shooting line
   d. Stand behind the shooting line with both feet

_____ 10. When archers have finished shooting all of their arrows, what should they do?
   a. Step back behind the shooting line, waiting until adjacent archers at full draw have released
   b. Go to the target to retrieve arrows
   c. Ask the adjacent archer whether it is all right to step back
   d. Wait on the line until the instructor blows the whistle to step back

_____ 11. What type of stance tends to put the bow arm into a position closer to the path of the bowstring upon release?

    a. Open stance

    b. Closed stance

    c. Square stance

    d. Obtuse stance

_____ 12. Where should the pressure of the bow be felt on the bow hand?

    a. The tips of the thumb and four fingers

    b. The thumb

    c. The base of the fingers

    d. The V formed at the thumb and index finger

_____ 13. Which statement is true regarding the weight distribution of the stance?

    a. Weight should be on the back foot

    b. Weight should be evenly distributed

    c. With the feet shoulder width apart, 60% of the weight is on the back foot, and 40% on the front foot

    d. Weight should be distributed 70% to the front foot and 30% to the back foot

_____ 14. What is the correct position of the bowstring as seen by the archer at full draw?

    a. The string should run up and down the center of the bow limbs

    b. The string should run up and down the left side of the limbs

    c. The string should run up and down the right side of the limbs

    d. The string should run up and down the right side of the bow and be about 1 inch from the side of the bow

_____ 15. Which statement describes the correct position of the draw hand in the anchor position?

    a. The back of the draw hand is cupped

    b. The back of the draw hand points upward

    c. The back of the draw hand is flat and relaxed

    d. The wrist of the draw hand is bent back (hyperextended) slightly

_____ 16. If an arrow barely touches the line between the red and the gold scoring rings of a target, what is the arrow's value?

    a. 9 points

    b. 8 points

    c. 7 points

    d. 6 points

_____ 17. Primarily which muscles should be used to draw a bow?

    a. Chest muscles

    b. Arm muscles

    c. Forearm muscles

    d. Back muscles

_____ 18. What is the name of the leather or vinyl piece of archery tackle that is worn to protect the bow arm from the bowstring?

    a. Arm guard

    b. Tab

    c. Cable guard

    d. Wrist sling

_____ 19. What is the pattern that arrows form on the target face called?

    a. Trajectory

    b. Grouping

    c. Spacing

    d. Dispersion

_____ 20. If all 6 arrows shot in an end land horizontally to the right of the bull's-eye, how are they described?

    a. As being at 9 o'clock

    b. As being at 3 o'clock

    c. As being off-center

    d. As being at right error

_____ 21. What do you call the part of the bow that is directly above the grip and is cut out to allow the arrow to sit close to the center of the bow?

    a. The bridge

    b. The sight window

    c. The skirt

    d. The pressure point

_____ 22. What is the actual draw weight of a bow that is marked 30 pounds and is shot by an archer whose draw length is 30 inches?

    a. 30 pounds

    b. Less than 30 pounds

    c. More than 30 pounds

    d. It cannot be determined

_____ 23. What is the distance from the pivot point to the bowstring (when the bow is braced or strung) called?

    a. Brace or string height

    b. Pivot height

    c. Draw length

    d. Cast

_____ 24. Bows made the transition from weapons to sport implements in

    a. The 800s B.C.

    b. The 1100s

    c. The 1500s

    d. The 1800s

_____ 25. What is the purpose of a stabilizer?

    a. It is an aiming device

    b. It is a foot rest for the bow

    c. It levels the bow

    d. It reduces the turning of the bow in the archer's bow hand

_____ 26. Which type of bow allows archers to hold only a fraction of the bow's draw weight at full draw?

    a. The straight-limb bow

    b. The compound bow

    c. The recurve bow

    d. The cross bow

_____ 27. Which anchor position has the advantage that it can be quickly established?

    a. The side anchor

    b. The behind-the-neck anchor

    c. The behind-the-ear anchor

    d. The under-chin anchor

_____ 28. Which bow hand position does not require great wrist strength for extended shooting sessions?

    a. The straight wrist

    b. The low wrist

    c. The flexed wrist

    d. The high wrist

_____ 29. What should the archer concentrate on after anchoring and checking bow and string-sight alignment?

    a. Any hand and arm positions that feel awkward

    b. How the wind is gusting

    c. Aiming

    d. Releasing before adjacent archers draw

_____ 30. What adjustment is necessary to correct for porpoising of an arrow shaft in flight?

    a. Tension of the plunger button

    b. Distance of the plunger button through the bow handle

    c. Length of the bowstring

    d. Position of the nock locator

_____ 31. Which of the following equipment acquisitions should come first?

    a. Aluminum arrows in a shaft size appropriate for the arrow length and bow weight

    b. A take-down recurve bow

    c. A tournament-quality bowsight

    d. An arrow rest with a cushion plunger

_____ 32. Which of the following is *not* an adjustment usually made by bowhunters?

    a.  Using a compound bow

    b.  Using a bowsight with several pins set for various distances

    c.  Adding a stabilizer of at least 30 inches

    d.  Camouflaging the bow and its accessories

*Labeling Directions*: Please label the parts of the bow and arrow illustrated by writing the appropriate name next to the number below that corresponds to the number on the illustration.

| _____ 1. | _____ 6. | _____ 11. | _____ 16. |
| _____ 2. | _____ 7. | _____ 12. | _____ 17. |
| _____ 3. | _____ 8. | _____ 13. | _____ 18. |
| _____ 4. | _____ 9. | _____ 14. | _____ 19. |
| _____ 5. | _____ 10. | _____ 15. | _____ 20. |

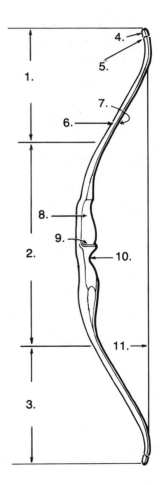

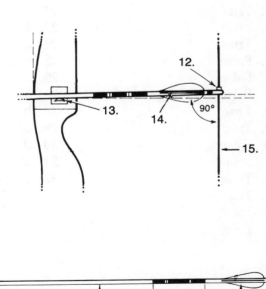

## WRITTEN EXAMINATION ANSWERS

*True/*
*False*

1. False
2. False
3. True
4. True
5. True
6. False
7. False
8. False
9. False
10. True
11. False
12. True
13. True
14. True
15. True
16. False
17. False
18. False
19. True
20. False
21. False
22. True
23. True
24. True
25. False
26. False
27. False
28. True
29. True
30. False
31. False
32. True
33. True
34. False
35. False

*Multiple*
*Choice*

1. c
2. d
3. a
4. b
5. c
6. b
7. a
8. a
9. c
10. a
11. b
12. d
13. b
14. a
15. c
16. a
17. d
18. a
19. b
20. b
21. b
22. c
23. a
24. c
25. d
26. b
27. a
28. b
29. c
30. d
31. a
32. c

*Labeling*

1. Upper limb/top limb
2. Handle riser
3. Lower limb/bottom limb
4. Tip
5. String notch
6. Back
7. Face
8. Sight window
9. Shelf
10. Pivot point
11. String
12. Nock locator
13. Arrow rest
14. Index feather
15. Serving
16. Point
17. Shaft
18. Fletching
19. Crest
20. Nock

# *Appendices*

A    Knowledge Structure of Archery (Overview)
B    Constructing Target Stands and an Arrow Cart
C    Constructing a Box Bow Stringer
D.1 Sample Scope and Teaching Sequence
D.2 Scope and Teaching Sequence (Blank)
E.1 Sample Individual Program
E.2 Individual Program (Blank)
F.1 Sample Lesson Plan
F.2 Lesson Plan (Blank)

# Appendix A
## How to Use the Knowledge Structure (Overview)

A knowledge structure is an instructional tool—by completing one you make a very personal statement about what you know about a subject and how that knowledge guides your decisions in teaching and coaching. The knowledge structure for archery outlined here has been designed for a teaching environment, with teaching progressions that emphasize technique and performance objectives in realistic settings. In a coaching environment, you would need to emphasize more physiological and conditioning factors, with training progressions that prepare athletes for competition.

The Knowledge Structure of Archery shows the first page or an *overview* of a completed knowledge structure. The knowledge structure is divided into broad categories of information that are used for all of the participant and instructor guides in the Steps to Success Activity Series. Those categories are:

- physiological training and conditioning,
- background knowledge,
- psychomotor skills and tactics, and
- psycho-social concepts.

Physiological training and conditioning has several subcategories, including warm-up and conditioning. Research in exercise physiology and the medical sciences has demonstrated the importance of warming up before physical activity. Minimal conditioning through strength exercises for the upper torso also may be necessary for your beginning archers. The participant and instructor guides present principles and exercises for effective warm-up and conditioning, which, because of time restrictions, are usually the only training activities done in the teaching environment. In a more intense coaching environment, additional categories should be added—weight-training principles, injury prevention, training progressions, and nutrition.

The background-knowledge category outlines subcategories of essential background knowledge that all instructors should have mastery of when beginning a class. For archery, background knowledge includes playing the game, basic rules/safety, equipment, and archery today.

Under psychomotor skills and tactics, all the individual skills in an activity are named. For archery, these are shown as the stance, bow hold, string hook, draw, anchor, aim, release, and follow-through. These skills are also presented in a recommended order of presentation. In a completed knowledge structure, each skill is broken down into subskills, delineating selected technical, biomechanical, motor learning, and other teaching and coaching points that describe mature performance. These points can be found in the Keys to Success and the Keys to Success Checklists in the participant book.

Once individual skills are identified and analyzed, selected basic adaptations of the activity are presented and analyzed. For archery these are identified as equipment, target size, distance, and forms.

The psycho-social category identifies selected concepts from the sport psychology and sociology literature that have been shown to contribute to learners' understanding of and success in the activity. These concepts are built into the key concepts and the activities for teaching. For archery, the concepts identified are relaxation, concentration, confidence, and visualization.

To be a successful teacher or coach, you must convert what you have learned as a student or done as a player or perfomer to knowledge that is conscious and appropriate for presentation to others. A knowledge structure is a tool designed to help you with this transition and to speed your *steps to success*. You should view a knowledge structure as the most basic level of teaching knowledge you possess for a sport or activity. For more information on how to develop your own knowledge structure, see the textbook that accompanies this series, *Instructional Design for Teaching Physical Activities*.

# Knowledge Structure of Archery (Overview)

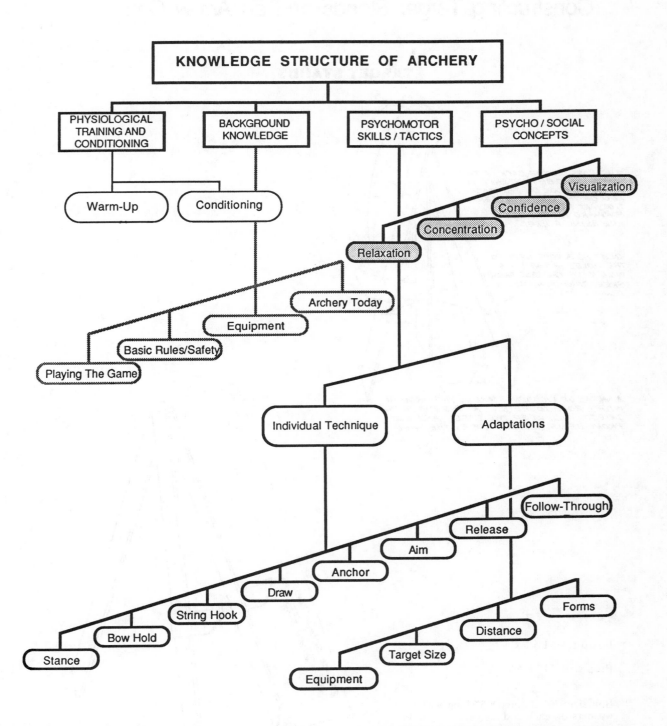

*Note.* From "The Role of Expert Knowledge Structures in an Instructional Design Model for Physical Education" by J.N. Vickers, 1983, *Journal of Teaching in Physical Education*, **2**(3), pp. 25, 27. Copyright 1983 by Joan N. Vickers. Adapted by permission. This Knowledge Structure of Archery was designed specifically for the Steps to Success Activity Series by Joan N. Vickers, Judy P. Wright, Kathleen M. Haywood, and Catherine F. Lewis.

# *Appendix B*
## Constructing Target Stands and an Arrow Cart

### TARGET STANDS

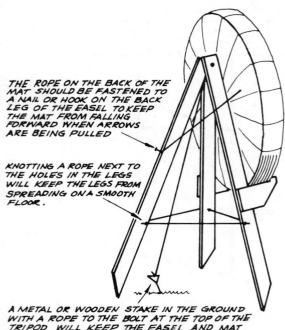

THE ROPE ON THE BACK OF THE
MAT SHOULD BE FASTENED TO
A NAIL OR HOOK ON THE BACK
LEG OF THE EASEL TO KEEP
THE MAT FROM FALLING
FORWARD WHEN ARROWS
ARE BEING PULLED

KNOTTING A ROPE NEXT TO
THE HOLES IN THE LEGS
WILL KEEP THE LEGS FROM
SPREADING ON A SMOOTH
FLOOR.

A METAL OR WOODEN STAKE IN THE GROUND
WITH A ROPE TO THE BOLT AT THE TOP OF THE
TRIPOD WILL KEEP THE EASEL AND MAT
FROM BEING BLOWN OVER BY THE WIND.

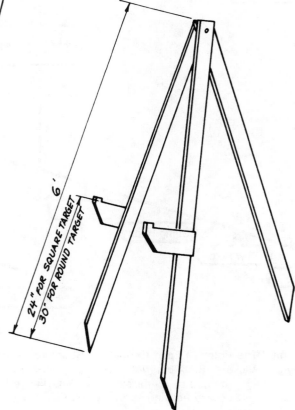

6'

24" FOR SQUARE TARGET
30" FOR ROUND TARGET

Board size: 1¼″ x 4″

Prop size: 11″ x 5″

Bolt size: ½″ diameter 5″ long with
washers on each end

# ARROW CART

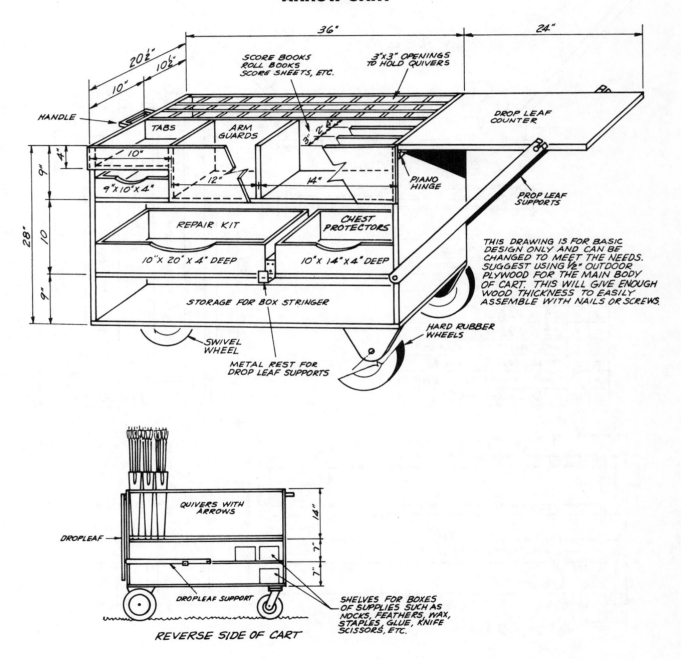

*Note.* From *The National Archery Association instructor's manual* (3rd ed.) (pp. 95, 97, 100) by Patricia Baier, Julia Bowers, C.R. Fowkes, and Sherwood Schoch. Edited by Ruth E. Rowe. Drawings by James E. Palmer. 1982, Colorado Springs: The National Archery Association of the United States. Copyright 1982 by the National Archery Association. Reprinted by permission.

# Appendix C
## Constructing a Box Bow Stringer

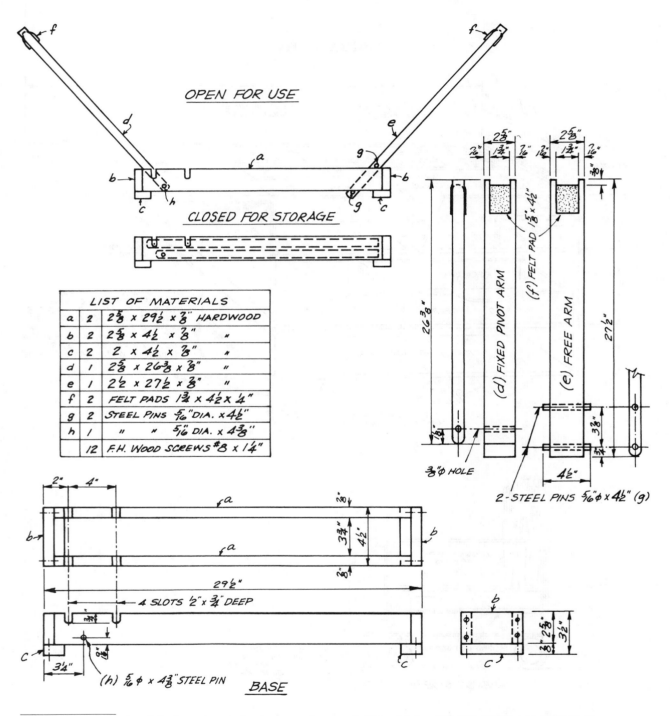

| | | LIST OF MATERIALS |
|---|---|---|
| a | 2 | $2\frac{5}{8}$ x $29\frac{1}{2}$ x $\frac{7}{8}$" HARDWOOD |
| b | 2 | $2\frac{5}{8}$ x $4\frac{1}{2}$ x $\frac{7}{8}$"      " |
| c | 2 | 2 x $4\frac{1}{2}$ x $\frac{7}{8}$"      " |
| d | 1 | $2\frac{5}{8}$ x $26\frac{3}{8}$ x $\frac{7}{8}$"      " |
| e | 1 | $2\frac{1}{2}$ x $27\frac{1}{2}$ x $\frac{7}{8}$"      " |
| f | 2 | FELT PADS $1\frac{3}{4}$ x $4\frac{1}{2}$ x $\frac{1}{4}$" |
| g | 2 | STEEL PINS $\frac{5}{16}$"DIA. x $4\frac{1}{2}$" |
| h | 1 |    "    "    $\frac{5}{16}$ DIA. x $4\frac{3}{8}$" |
| | 12 | F.H. WOOD SCREWS #8 x $1\frac{1}{4}$" |

*Note.* From *The National Archery Association instructor's manual* (3rd ed.) (pp. 95, 97, 100) by Patricia Baier, Julia Bowers, C.R. Fowkes, and Sherwood Schoch. Edited by Ruth E. Rowe. Drawings by James E. Palmer. 1982, Colorado Springs: The National Archery Association of the United States. Copyright 1982 by the National Archery Association. Reprinted by permission.

# Appendix D.1

## Sample Scope and Teaching Sequence

NAME OF ACTIVITY: Archery
LEVEL OF LEARNER: Beginning

Legend: N = New   R = Review   C = Continue   P = Student Directed Practice

| Steps | Session Number | 1 | 2 | 3 | 4 | 5 | 6 | 7 | 8 | 9 | 10 | 11 | 12 | 13 | 14 | 15 | 16 | 17 | 18 | 19 | 20 | 21 | 22 | 23 | 24 | 25 | 26 | 27 | 28 | 29 | 30 |
|---|---|---|---|---|---|---|---|---|---|---|---|---|---|---|---|---|---|---|---|---|---|---|---|---|---|---|---|---|---|---|---|
| 1 | Fitting equipment | N | | | | | | | | | | | | | | | | | | | | | | | | | | | | | |
| 2 | Safety | | N | R | | | | | | | | | | | | | | | | | | | | | | | | | | | |
| 3 | Mimicking | | N | R | | | | | | | | | | | | | | | | | | | | | | | | | | | |
| 4 | Shooting form | | N | P | P | | | | | | | | | | | | | | | | | | | | | | | | | | |
| 5 | Improving accuracy | | | | N | P | P | | | | | | | | | | | | | | | | | | | | | | | | |
| 6 | Adding accessories | | | | | | | N | | | | | | | | | | | | | | | | | | | | | | | |
| 7 | Using a bowsight | | | | | | | N | P | P | P | | | | | | | | | | | | | | | | | | | | |
| 8 | Correcting errors | | | | | | | | | | | N | C | C | | | | | | | | | | | | | | | | | |
| 9 | Varying stance | | | | | | | | | | | | | | N | R | | | | | | | | | | | | | | | |
| 10 | Bow hand position | | | | | | | | | | | | | | | N | R | | | | | | | | | | | | | | |
| 11 | Anchor position | | | | | | | | | | | | | | | | N | R | | | | | | | | | | | | | |
| 12 | Mental checklist | | | | | | | | | | | | | | | | | N | P | P | | | | | | | | | | | |
| 13 | Scoring | | | | | | | | | | | | | | | | | | N | R | | | | | | | | | | | |
| 14 | Tournament shooting | | | | | | | | | | | | | | | | | | | | N | C | C | C | C | C | C | | | | |
| 15 | Mental approach | | | | | | | | | | | | | | | | | | | | | | | N | R | P | P | | | | |
| 16 | Tuning equipment | | | | | | | | | | | | | | | | | | | | | | | | | | | N | R | | |
| 17 | Maintaining equipment | | | | | | | | | | | | | | | | | | | | | | | | | | | | N | R | |
| 18 | Upgrading equipment | | | | | | | | | | | | | | | | | | | | | | | | | | | | | N | |
| 19 | | | | | | | | | | | | | | | | | | | | | | | | | | | | | | | |
| 20 | | | | | | | | | | | | | | | | | | | | | | | | | | | | | | | |
| 21 | | | | | | | | | | | | | | | | | | | | | | | | | | | | | | | |
| 22 | | | | | | | | | | | | | | | | | | | | | | | | | | | | | | | |
| 23 | | | | | | | | | | | | | | | | | | | | | | | | | | | | | | | |
| 24 | | | | | | | | | | | | | | | | | | | | | | | | | | | | | | | |
| 25 | | | | | | | | | | | | | | | | | | | | | | | | | | | | | | | |

# *Appendix D.2*

## How to Use the Scope and Teaching Sequence Form

A completed Scope and Teaching Sequence is, in effect, a master lesson plan. It lists all the individual skills to be included in your course, recorded (vertically) in the progressive sequence in which you have decided to present them and showing (horizontally) the manner and the sessions in which you will teach them.

The Sample Scope and Teaching Sequence (Appendix D.1) illustrates how the chart is to be used. This chart indicates that in session 15 the class will review stance variations and will try various bow hand positions for the first time. It also indicates that the skills in Step 4, for example, are worked on for three sessions—one introduction and two practice sessions.

A course Scope and Teaching Sequence (using the blank form in Appendix D.2) will help you to better plan your daily teaching strategies (see Appendix F.2). It will take some experience to predict accurately how much material you can cover in each session, but by completing a plan like this, you can compare your progress to your plan and revise the plan to better fit the next class.

The chart will also help you tailor the amount of material to the length of time you have to teach it. Notice that this particular sample indicates that 30 sessions are needed to cover the 18 steps. Some skills would have to be eliminated if fewer sessions are available. Be sure that your course's Scope and Teaching Sequence allots ample time for review and practice of each area.

# Scope and Teaching Sequence

New N   Review R   Continue C   Student Directed Practice P

NAME OF ACTIVITY _____

LEVEL OF LEARNER _____

| Steps | Session Number | 1 | 2 | 3 | 4 | 5 | 6 | 7 | 8 | 9 | 10 | 11 | 12 | 13 | 14 | 15 | 16 | 17 | 18 | 19 | 20 | 21 | 22 | 23 | 24 | 25 | 26 | 27 | 28 | 29 | 30 |
|---|---|---|---|---|---|---|---|---|---|---|---|---|---|---|---|---|---|---|---|---|---|---|---|---|---|---|---|---|---|---|---|
| 1 | | | | | | | | | | | | | | | | | | | | | | | | | | | | | | | | |
| 2 | | | | | | | | | | | | | | | | | | | | | | | | | | | | | | | | |
| 3 | | | | | | | | | | | | | | | | | | | | | | | | | | | | | | | | |
| 4 | | | | | | | | | | | | | | | | | | | | | | | | | | | | | | | | |
| 5 | | | | | | | | | | | | | | | | | | | | | | | | | | | | | | | | |
| 6 | | | | | | | | | | | | | | | | | | | | | | | | | | | | | | | | |
| 7 | | | | | | | | | | | | | | | | | | | | | | | | | | | | | | | | |
| 8 | | | | | | | | | | | | | | | | | | | | | | | | | | | | | | | | |
| 9 | | | | | | | | | | | | | | | | | | | | | | | | | | | | | | | | |
| 10 | | | | | | | | | | | | | | | | | | | | | | | | | | | | | | | | |
| 11 | | | | | | | | | | | | | | | | | | | | | | | | | | | | | | | | |
| 12 | | | | | | | | | | | | | | | | | | | | | | | | | | | | | | | | |
| 13 | | | | | | | | | | | | | | | | | | | | | | | | | | | | | | | | |
| 14 | | | | | | | | | | | | | | | | | | | | | | | | | | | | | | | | |
| 15 | | | | | | | | | | | | | | | | | | | | | | | | | | | | | | | | |
| 16 | | | | | | | | | | | | | | | | | | | | | | | | | | | | | | | | |
| 17 | | | | | | | | | | | | | | | | | | | | | | | | | | | | | | | | |
| 18 | | | | | | | | | | | | | | | | | | | | | | | | | | | | | | | | |
| 19 | | | | | | | | | | | | | | | | | | | | | | | | | | | | | | | | |
| 20 | | | | | | | | | | | | | | | | | | | | | | | | | | | | | | | | |
| 21 | | | | | | | | | | | | | | | | | | | | | | | | | | | | | | | | |
| 22 | | | | | | | | | | | | | | | | | | | | | | | | | | | | | | | | |
| 23 | | | | | | | | | | | | | | | | | | | | | | | | | | | | | | | | |
| 24 | | | | | | | | | | | | | | | | | | | | | | | | | | | | | | | | |
| 25 | | | | | | | | | | | | | | | | | | | | | | | | | | | | | | | | |

Notes:

# Appendix E.1

## Sample Individual Program

INDIVIDUAL COURSE IN _____     GRADE/COURSE SECTION _____

STUDENT'S NAME _____     STUDENT ID # _____

| SKILLS/CONCEPTS | TECHNIQUE AND PERFORMANCE OBJECTIVES | WT* × | POINT PROGRESS** | | | | = FINAL SCORE*** |
|---|---|---|---|---|---|---|---|
| | | | 1 | 2 | 3 | 4 | |
| 1 Stance Technique | Straddles line; weight even, consistent position; aligned with target; body erect. | 1.0 | | | | | |
| 2 Nocking Technique | Arrow oriented correctly, against nock locator | 1.0 | | | | | |
| 3 Bow Hand and Arm Technique | Consistent hand placement; handle in V of hand; hand relaxed; elbow rotated | 1.0 | | | | | |
| 4 Draw Technique | 3-finger hook; back of draw hand flat, relaxed; elbow back first; elbow at shoulder level; shoulders level, aligned to target | 1.5 | | | | | |
| 5 Anchor Technique | Positioned properly; consistent; teeth together; kisser button positioned | 1.0 | | | | | |
| 6 Aim Technique | Bow level; correct eye used; string aligned; archer settles and holds | 1.0 | | | | | |
| 7 Release Technique | By relaxing hook; head steady; bow hand and arm steady | 1.5 | | | | | |
| 8 Follow-Through Technique | Head steady; bow arm up and toward target; draw hand over rear shoulder | 1.5 | | | | | |
| 9 Basic Shooting Form Performance (Step 4) | Number out of 18 arrows landing on 2 ft × 2 ft paper from 10 yds (without sight) | 1.0 | 6 | 10 | 14 | 18 | |
| 10 Improved Shooting Form Performance (Step 5) | Score for 4 six-arrow ends at 80-cm 10-ring target from 10 yds (without sight) | 1.0 | 48 | 96 | 144 | 192 | |

| # | Objective | Description | WT | | | | | |
|---|-----------|-------------|----|----|----|----|----|----|
| 11 | Sight Shooting Performance (Step 7) | Score for 4 six-arrow ends at 80-cm 10-ring target from 20 yds (with sight) | 1.0 | 48 | 96 | 144 | 192 | |
| 12 | Individualized Form Performance (Step 11) | Score for 4 six-arrow ends shot at 80-cm 10-ring target from each distance: 30, 20, 10 yds | 1.5 | 144 | 288 | 432 | 576 | |
| 13 | Tournament Shooting Performance (Step 14) | Modified Metric 900 Round (Step 14, Drill 1) | 1.5 | 180 | 360 | 540 | 720 | |
| 14 | Tournament Shooting Performance (Step 14) | Modified Interscholastic Metric Round (Step 14, Drill 2) | 1.5 | 144 | 288 | 432 | 576 | |
| 15 | Error Analysis Technique | Identification of likely errors through arrow pattern analysis | 1.5 | | | | | |
| 16 | Mental Approach | Concentrates; maintains relaxation | 1.0 | | | | | |
| 17 | Goal Setting | Ability to set realistic goals; confident of attaining goals | 1.0 | | | | | |
| 18 | Written Exam | Value = 20% | | | | | | |

TOTAL = 100%

*WT = Weighting of an objective's degree of difficulty.

**PROGRESS = Ongoing success, which may be expressed in terms of (a) accumulated points (1, 2, 3, 4); (b) grades (D, C, B, A); (c) symbols (merit, bronze, silver, gold); (d) unsatisfactory/satisfactory; and others as desired.

***FINAL SCORE equals WT times PROGRESS.

# Appendix E.2

## Individual Program

INDIVIDUAL COURSE IN _____

STUDENT'S NAME _____

GRADE/COURSE SECTION _____

STUDENT ID # _____

| SKILLS/CONCEPTS | TECHNIQUE AND PERFORMANCE OBJECTIVES | WT* × PROGRESS** = | 1 | 2 | 3 | 4 | FINAL SCORE*** |
|---|---|---|---|---|---|---|---|
| | | | | | | | |
| | | | | | | | |
| | | | | | | | |
| | | | | | | | |
| | | | | | | | |
| | | | | | | | |

*Note.* From "The Role of Expert Knowledge Structures in an Instructional Design Model for Physical Education" by J.N. Vickers, 1983, *Journal of Teaching in Physical Education*, 2(3), p. 17. Copyright 1983 by Joan N. Vickers. Adapted by permission.

*WT = Weighting of an objective's degree of difficulty.

**PROGRESS = Ongoing success, which may be expressed in terms of (a) accumulated points (1, 2, 3, 4); (b) grades (D, C, B, A); (c) symbols (merit, bronze, silver, gold); (d) unsatisfactory/satisfactory; and others as desired.

***FINAL SCORE equals WT times PROGRESS.

# Appendix E.2
## How to Use the Individual Program Form

To complete an individual program for each student, you must first make five decisions about evaluation:

1. How many skills or concepts can you or should you evaluate, considering the number of students and the time available? The larger your classes and the shorter your class length, the fewer objectives you will be able to use.
2. What specific quantitative or qualitative criteria will you use to evaluate specific skills? See the Sample Individual Program (Appendix E.1) for ideas.
3. What relative weight is to be assigned to each specific skill, considering its importance in the course and the amount of practice time available?
4. What type of grading system do you wish to use? Will you use letters (A, B, C, D), satisfactory/unsatisfactory, a number or point system (1, 2, 3, etc.), or percentages (10%, 20%, 30%, etc.)? Or you may prefer a system of achievement levels, such as colors (red, white, blue), or medallions (gold, silver, bronze).
5. Who will do the evaluating? You may want to delegate certain quantitative evaluations to be made by the students' peers, up to a predetermined skill level (e.g., a "B" grade), with all qualitative evaluations and all top-grade determinations being made by you.

Once you have made these decisions, draw up an evaluation sheet (using Appendix E.2) that will fit the majority of your class members. Then decide whether you will establish a minimum level as a passing/failing point. Calculate the minimum passing score and the maximum attainable score, and divide the difference into as many grade categories as you wish. If you use an achievement-level system, assign a numerical value to each level for your calculations.

The blank Individual Program sheet, as shown in Appendix E.2, is intended not to be used verbatim (although you may do so if you wish), but rather to suggest ideas that you can use, adapt, and integrate with your own ideas to tailor your program to you and your students.

Make copies of your program evaluation system to hand out to each student at your first class meeting, and be prepared to make modifications for those who need special consideration. Such modifications could be changing the weight assigned to particular skills for certain students, or emphasizing some skills over others, or varying the criteria used for evaluating selected students. Thus, individual differences can be recognized within your class.

You, the instructor, have the freedom to make the decisions about evaluating your students. Be creative. The best teachers always are.

# *Appendix F.1*

## Sample Lesson Plan

Lesson plan _____3_____ of _____28_____ Activity: ___Archery___

Class ___Archery___

S = Student; T = Teacher

Objectives:
1. Review the mimicked shot
2. Review the basic shot
3. Improve technique in executing the basic shot
4. Achieve feeling of comfort in handling equipment

| Skill or concept | Learning activity | Teaching points | Time (min) |
|---|---|---|---|
| 1. Distribute equipment | | • Get your equipment as soon as you arrive for class | 2 |
| 2. Introduction/outline objectives | | | 1 |
| 3. Teach warm-up | • Running in place | | 2 |
| | • Stretching | | 2 |
| | • Strength exercises (distribute/collect exercise tubing) | | 2 |
| 4. Mimicking review | • Redemonstrate mimicking shot with bow, no arrow | • Review major cues<br>Side to target<br>Feet aligned, weight even<br>Stand straight<br>Bow hand with bow in V<br>Set hook<br>Raise bow, rotate elbow<br>Elbow back<br>Chin on hand, string on chin, nose<br>Ease string back | 5 |
| | • Cue 12 repetitions<br><br>SSSS SSSS SSSS SSSS<br>T<br><br>targets | | |

| | | | |
|---|---|---|---|
| 5. Basic shot review | • Redemonstrate basic shot<br>• Cue practice, 1 end<br><br>T<br><br>SSSS SSSS SSSS SSSS<br><br>targets (10 yards) | • Review major cues<br>  Stance<br>  Against nock locator<br>  Index feather toward<br>    you<br>  One finger above,<br>    2 below nock<br>  Raise bow, rotate<br>    elbow<br>  Draw elbow back<br>  Anchor, tighten back<br>  Relax hand to release | 5 |
| 6. Shooting drill | • Two 6-arrow ends from 10 yd at 12-inch paper plate | • Correct errors as needed | 10 |
| 7. Scoring drill | • One end for standard<br>• Four ends for score<br>• From 10 yd at 2 ft × 2 ft paper | | 18 |
| 8. Store equipment | | | 2 |

# Appendix F.2
## How to Use the Lesson Plan Form

All teachers have learned in their training that lesson plans are vital to good teaching. This is a commonly accepted axiom, but there are many variations in the form that lesson plans can take.

An effective lesson plan sets forth the objectives to be attained or attempted during the session. If there is no objective, then there is no reason for teaching, and no basis for judging whether the teaching is effective.

Once you have named your objectives, list specific activities that will lead to attaining each. Every activity must be described in detail—what will take place and in what order, and how the class will be organized for the optimum learning situation. Record key words or phrases as focal points as well as, particularly in archery, brief reminders of the applicable safety precautions.

Finally, set a time schedule that allocates a segment of the lesson for each activity to guide you in keeping to your plan. It is wise to also include in your lesson plan a list of all the equipment you will need, as a reminder to check for availability of the shooting range and location of the equipment before class.

An organized, professional approach to teaching requires preparing daily lesson plans. Each lesson plan provides you with an effective overview of your intended instruction and a means to evaluate it when class is over. Having lesson plans on file allows someone else to teach in your absence.

You may modify the blank Lesson Plan shown in Appendix F.2 to fit your own needs. For example, you could modify it to include an equipment list or add specific opening and closing points for your lesson.

# Lesson Plan

| LESSON PLAN _____ OF _____ | | OBJECTIVES: | |
| --- | --- | --- | --- |
| ACTIVITY _____ | | | |
| CLASS _____ | | | |

| SKILL OR CONCEPT | LEARNING ACTIVITIES | TEACHING POINTS | TIME |
| --- | --- | --- | --- |
| | | | |

*Note.* From *Badminton: A Structures of Knowledge Approach* (p. 95) by J.N. Vickers and D. Brecht, 1987, Calgary, AB: University Printing Services. Copyright 1987 by Joan N. Vickers. Reprinted by permission.

# References

Baier, P., Bowers, J., Fowkes, C.R., & Schoch, S. (1982). *The National Archery Association instructor's manual* (3rd ed.). Colorado Springs, CO: National Archery Association of the United States.

Bavousett, F., & Beardsley, M. (1979). *Archery lab manual*. College Station, TX: Unlimited Products.

Easton Aluminum Co. (1981). *Target archery with Easton Aluminum Shafts*. Van Nuys, CA: Author.

Goc-Karp, G. , & Zakrajsek, D.B. (1987). Planning for learning: Theory into practice. *Journal of Teaching in Physical Education*, 6(4), 377-392.

Housner, L.D., & Griffey, D.C. (1985). Teacher cognition: Differences in planning and interactive decision making between experienced and inexperienced teachers. *Research Quarterly for Exercise and Sport*, 56(1), 45-53.

Imwold, C.H., & Hoffman, S.J. (1983). Visual recognition of a gymnastic skill by experienced and inexperienced instructors. *Research Quarterly for Exercise and Sport*, 54(2), 149-155.

Klann, M.L. (1970). *Target archery*. Reading, MA: Addison-Wesley.

McKinney, W.C., & McKinney, M.W. (1985). *Archery*. Dubuque, IA: William C. Brown.

Paterson, W.F. (1984). *Encyclopaedia of archery*. New York: St. Martin's Press.

Williams, J.C. (1985). *Archery for beginners* (2nd ed.). Chicago, IL: Contemporary Books.

Wise, L. (1985). *Tuning your compound bow*. Mequon, WI: Target Communications.

# Suggested Readings

American Association for Health, Physical Education, and Recreation. (1972). *Archery: A planning guide for group and individual instruction*. Washington, DC: Author.

Baier, P., Bowers, J., Fowkes, C.R., & Schoch, S. (1982). *The National Archery Association instructor's manual* (3rd ed.). Colorado Springs, CO: National Archery Association of the United States.

Barrett, J.A. (1973). *Archery* (2nd ed.). Pacific Palisades, CA: Goodyear Publishing.

Bavousett, F.L. (1979). *Beginning target archery*. College Station, TX: Unlimited Products.

Easton Aluminum Co. (1981). *Target archery with Easton Aluminum Shafts*. Van Nuys, CA: Author.

Hadas, L. (1980). *Champions*. Panorama City, CA: L.F.H. Film Production.

Henderson, A. (1983). *Understanding winning archery*. Mequon, WI: Target Communications.

Keaggy, D., Sr. (1968). *Power archery* (2nd ed.). Drayton Plains, MI: Power Archery Products.

Klann, M.L. (1970).*Target archery*. Reading, MA: Addison-Wesley.

McKinney, W.C., & McKinney, M.W. (1985). *Archery*. Dubuque, IA: William C. Brown.

Paterson, W.F. (1984). *Encyclopaedia of archery*. New York: St. Martin's Press.

Williams, J.C. (1985). *Archery for beginners* (2nd ed.). Chicago, IL: Contemporary Books.

Wise, L. (1985). *Tuning your compound bow*. Mequon, WI: Target Communications.

## Periodical

*The U.S. Archer*. 7315 North San Anna Drive, Tucson, AZ 85704.

# About the Authors

Kathleen M. Haywood, PhD, is associate professor of physical education at the University of Missouri-St. Louis and is a member of the Professional Archers Association and the professional division of the National Field Archery Association. On the professional tour she is sponsored by the Ludwikoski-Wortman distributors of Golden Eagle bows and is a member of the Saunders Archery Company product-testing team.

An eight-time Missouri state champion, in 1985 Dr. Haywood was both the indoor and outdoor Midwest Sectional champion of the National Field Archery Association. In addition to giving private instruction, she has taught archery at Washington University and the University of Illinois. Widely published in such journals as *Research Quarterly for Exercise and Sport*, the *British Journal of Sports Medicine*, the *Journal of Sport Sciences*, and the *Journal of Motor Behavior*, Dr. Haywood is also the author of *Life Span Motor Development* (Human Kinetic Publishers, 1986). Her recreational activities include jogging, softball, and tennis.

Catherine F. Lewis, MEd, teaches elementary physical education at the Andrews Academy in Creve Coeur, Missouri. In 1983 she was the Midwest Sectional indoor champion of the National Field Archery Association, belonging to that group's professional division as well as the Professional Archers Association. Ms. Lewis is an exceptional teacher, having taught archery in the professional preparation program at the University of Missouri-St. Louis and to youths in school, scouting, and camp programs. When not teaching or entered in archery competitions, she devotes her leisure time to softball, camping, and fishing.